New Angles on Golf

New Angles on Golf

by an amateur
for serious amateurs

George Rothman

Foreword by Peter Alliss

To Rosie, my occasional golf partner
and wonderful wife of 51 years

30% of the author's gross receipts from
sales of this book will be donated to
Cancer Research UK

First published 2010 by
JJG Publishing
Sparrow Hall
Hindringham
Fakenham
Norfolk NR21 0DP

Distributed through the book trade
by Quiller Publishing Ltd.

Copyright © 2010 George Rothman

ISBN 978-1-899163-94-6

Printed in China through Colorcraft Ltd., Hong Kong

Contents

Foreword by Peter Alliss

Ihave been surprised by my willingness to recommend an instructional golf book written by
an amateur, but George is very different. *New
Angles On Golf* gives sound advice on techniques,
but it is also packed with fascinating nuggets of in-
formation, personal asides about the world of golf,
and it includes many of George's learning curve ex-
periences and perceptive views on the game he
loves.

A single figure golfer for fifty-seven years,
George has read widely, and he has clearly
absorbed the theories of the great teachers of the
game. He has carefully included the tips that he
thinks will be of the greatest help to the aspiring
amateur, plus coming up with many new ideas of
his own, all very convincing, because they are from
personal experience.

The chapter on the benefits of positive thinking in
golf – as in life – rings very true, coming as it does
from someone who has impressively faced up to his
own health problems.

Well done George. It's a damned good read, and
you are a wonderful example of the true enthusiast.
I marvel at the time you must have spent on research for this imaginative and helpful book.

Acknowledgements

My warm thanks for their kind and patient help to:

Peter Alliss for his Foreword and for helping raise more for Cancer Research UK.

Dave Pelz. The Pelz Golf Organisation, in particular Carl Mickelson, for carefully checking through and approving all that I have written about them in my specific references to Dave Pelz's two books.

Golf Society of Great Britain and their book *Search for the Perfect Swing*. I've praised their work highly and am a long-standing member.

Professional advice. Martyn Landsborough, Senior Professional, Royal Ashdown Forest Golf Club, for reading my drafts and his helpful suggestions and making available Tim Cowley, Assistant Professional, for photos. Douglas Neave, Secretary, Royal Ashdown Forest Golf Club for use of tees etc. for photographic session.

Photo session. Fiona Brown, PGA Professional, Nick Champness and Tim Cowley for appearing in the photos, and Harry Rashleigh-Belcher for taking them.

Draft reading and suggestions. Old golfing friends for reading my many drafts, and for their candid criticisms and suggestions which have all helped. Nick Champness (Reigning and 7 times One-Armed World Champion), Duncan Ferguson (golf author), Maie Osborn, Charles Probett, James Rothman, Peter Roy (Mechanical Engineering), Brian Sennett, Charles Wade (sports journalist), David and Anne Wigglesworth.

Publishing advice and help. Roddy Bloomfield, top Sports Editor at Hodders, who has been exceptionally helpful and encouraging, Barry Gillions of Hamlyns, Jeremy Greenwood, my most patient and encouraging Publisher and Editor, Graham Hiles, Designer and Gill Jarrett, Editorial Assistant.

Cancer Research UK Charity. Hugo Middlemas for initial advice, and Natasha Etienne of CR UK.

Part I

Mostly technical

Chapter 1

Art or Science?

From many centuries ago when golf was first played in roughly its present form, the thoughts of the golfer about to play a shot have been similar to what they are today – how's the ball lying? where must I land it? what will it do after first hitting the ground? The early golfers relied mostly on judgement of distances by eye, instinct and local knowledge to work out how to play the next shot. On their home course they knew how far the ball would fly in the air from fixed points such as where their drive might typically finish, and what club they would normally hit from there. They fed in corrections instinctively for wind and temperature, the lie, slopes and the firmness of the ground on landing.

Improvements in the ball – the new more durable "gutty" replaced the "feathery" in 1850, and then the modern Haskell rubber-wound ball in 1900 – made the game more affordable and helped the explosion of course building from the 1880s, when courses started to penetrate inland more. Grassier fairways, increases in the number and variety of irons, and more lift on the ball flight made many long shots slightly more aerial, and less running. The instinctive approach continued, but by the 1960s golf had started to become more scientific:

pros now knew exact yardages that they needed to carry, or to lay up to behind hazards, and the distances their various clubs would carry in different conditions

A crucial development then was a research project undertaken for the Golf Society of Great Britain in the mid-1960s involving ten top British scientists, which resulted in *The Search for the Perfect Swing*, in 1968. Far ahead of its time, it was probably the first attempt to research scientifically not only the swing, but many other aspects of the game. It continues to be sold today, in precisely its original format: I know of no other comparable research study to this day. I accept and agree with almost all its work and conclusions. This 1968 book remains on the "Preferred Reading List" for professionals for both the PGA and the USPGA. Golf equipment and the condition of greens has changed since 1968, and these changes might have modified some of the science only a little. I discuss three of the huge number of topics in that book in Chapter 3 – "17 Common Conceptions questioned". CC 3 – "Straight left arm?" – its pros and cons, CC 4 – "Clubhead speed alone determines distance", and CC 5 – "After impact nothing can alter the outcome". I question some of the detail re CCs 4 and 5.

The other vital contribution to research in its very different way is David Pelz's work, starting with *Putt like the Pros* 1989, followed by *Dave Pelz's Short Game Bible* 1999, and *Dave Pelz's Putting Bible* 2000, which effectively supersedes his 1989 book on putting. Pelz, a former NASA physicist, started his research on golf in the mid 1970s. He quickly discovered among other things that while top pros were unsurprisingly accurate with their full shots, they were surprisingly bad with distance control of their part-strength wedges. The pros must have realized that their wedges at lesser distances were unreliable, and that they could get much better distance control from further away with full wedges.

Pelz, having recognized this problem, found a remedy. This is his "Finesse part-strength wedges system", which enables top pros, and potentially any golfer, to carry virtually any precise distance through the air. Since that time pros no longer *have to* lay back for full wedges. But variable spin is still a problem for them, often more so with a full wedge, but less so with a part-strength wedge, which can make approaching from nearer even more attractive. Pelz's system, which involves using at least 2, or preferably 3 or 4 wedges, and controlling distance by the length of the backswing, is described in Chapter 7 – "Pitching".

This book suggests ways forward for golf becoming even more scientific. It is bound to happen. There is scope for further advances in swing analysis using high speed cameras of at least 10,000 pictures per second, and impact analysis with very high speed digital cameras at speeds of up to millions of pictures per second. I do not know exactly how far club and ball manufacturers have yet gone down these routes. There is much complex technology in the club/ball contact – the elasticity of the ball, and of the clubface if it is a (metal) wood or "utility"; the whip and twist of the shaft during impact, the launch angles and spin rates, and the degree of off-centre contact. Club manufacturers can tune their

5

clubs' performance for different sectors of the market. For the golfer's movements, there could and should be more standardization in camera positions when filming the swing, and if body reference points were also marked on players one could see better what was happening, and make comparisons. A standardized grid might be superimposed by the camera accurately to measure the various movements. Strain gauges have already been used for many years to examine the forces involved at various key points.

At the same time I think it is a shame that some of the artistry is gradually being replaced by more and more science and calculation. I am sorry if this book will further speed that process. But however scientific it gets in years to come, there will remain a large amount of artistry, skill and instinct: and a very good thing too!

Chapter 2:

Instruction Books

There are a huge number of books that have been written about golf, many of them instructional. The oldest golf club in Italy – the delightful Menaggio and Cadenabbia GC, near Lake Como, founded in 1907 by a Scotsman – has a superb library of more than 5000 golf books. There are very many excellent instructional books and videos or DVDs, created by top players and teachers: I refer to a few of the books from my collection. The great teachers are often people who have been very good at the game, but have not maybe quite reached the topmost level. Because of this they might have been more aware of the problems in golf, and maybe thought about it a little more, so as to explain things to the ordinary performer. The top players who write books are brilliant at their playing skill, and they often collaborate with a professional writer to convey their ideas, mostly very effectively.

Some books tell you how to play the game at the top level – they don't always allow for the more ordinary golfer. They don't always set things out entirely clearly and unambiguously, or give reasons for doing something that way, or discuss the pros and cons of different methods. This book is *not a comprehensive instruction book*: I have left many deliberate gaps, which are partly filled by some of the books I have which I detail below. The only complete instruction manual is the Tiger Woods book *How I play Golf* 2001.

I have been greatly influenced by the three books I have discussed in Chapter 1 and which are by far the most important works of research to this day that I know of – *The Search for the Perfect Swing* 1968 and the two Pelz books *Dave Pelz's Short Game Bible* 1999, and *Dave Pelz's Putting Bible* 2000. Pelz has analysed all aspects of the short game from over 100 yards down, including all kinds of difficult situations. Each of his "Bibles" runs to about 400 pages, and tells you just about all you need to know on and close to the green. Peltz Golf work with very many top golfers and ordinary amateurs in their golf schools, on the Short game and Putting. I refer the reader to his books in the relevant chapters. I have checked my texts with Pelz Golf, who are happy with my interpretations of *Dave Pelz's Short Game Bible*, and *Dave Pelz's Putting Bible*, and my references to them throughout this book.

My recommended list from my own collection of 104 golf books:

1. *The Search for the Perfect Swing* 1968 by Alastair Cochran and John Stobbs, prepared and written for the Golf Society of Great Britain, Heinemann 434 14000 7, still available in identical 2005 edition with new Preface by Alastair Cochran; Triumph Books.

2. The 2 works by David Pelz: *Dave Pelz's Short*

game Bible 1999 Broadway Books ISBN 0-7679-0344-7 and *Dave Pelz's Putting Bible* 2000 – Doubleday ISBN 0-385-50024-6

Also thirteen other technical books I have by ten authors, which I recommend, listed alphabetically. I must have missed out a vast number of excellent books, but only because I do not own them.

Mindy Blake. *The Golf Swing of the Future* 1972 Souvenir Press, and *Golf: The Technique Barrier* 1978 Souvenir Press. Mindy Blake was a fine golfer, and was New Zealand Gymnastic and Pole Vault Champion. A Physics lecturer, he was a Squadron Commander in WW2, with DSO and DFC. Very knowledgeable on many aspects of golf, the swing he used himself and favoured was based on J H Taylor's action, which Blake claims was fundamentally sounder than modern methods. But Vardon's success with the "modern" swing when he just beat JH in a 36 hole play-off for the 1896 Open, made Vardon's swing the way forward. Blake invented and produced the "Swingrite".

Jim Flick. *Square-to-Square Golf in Pictures* 1974 Golf Digest. May be the definitive work on this subject. This method is at the heart of most of the accepted variations in golf swings today. It calls for little or no wrist-hinging or forearm rotation.

Ben Hogan. *The Modern Fundamentals of Golf* 1957 Nicholas Kaye. One of the greatest golf classics. Hogan was so successful at the long game that he commands enormous respect. He may have been the first to describe so vividly the sequence of events during the power swing as a "chain reaction" with each successive move kicking in at the right time.

John Jacobs. *Golf Doctor* 1979 Stanley Paul. Diagnosis, explanation and correction of golfing faults. Jacobs, Captain of the first ever European teams in the Ryder Cup in 1979 and 1981, is one of the world's most respected teachers. He offers remedies for 25 problems and guidance on 8 special situations.

Robert Trent Jones Jnr. *Golf by Design* 1993 Little, Brown – How to Lower Your Score by Reading the Features of a Course. I include this book in the "Technical Group", because it tells you how to read a golf course. Trent Jones Jr. is one of the most acclaimed Golf Course Architects of all time: he brilliantly tells you what the Architect tries to do to puzzle us and to make courses more interesting and challenging, and helps you to understand and interpret some of their skill, and improve your play accordingly.

David Leadbetter. Three books from maybe the best known of all the current teachers:

1. *The Golf Swing* 1990 Collins Willow. Deals with the "power swing". Not unlike Ben Hogan in principle, Leadbetter comes up with a series of movements in sequence, and shows you where things can go wrong.

2. *Faults and Fixes* 1993 Collins Willow. Leadbetter covers the whole game, and illustrates no less than 80 faults and how to correct them.

3. *Lessons from the Golf Greats* 1995 Collins Willow. Leadbetter takes twenty-five top pros from 1995 including two lady pros, and illustrates points from 8-shot swing sequences from in front and from down the line.

Arnold Palmer. *Golf Tactics* 1970 Kaye and Ward.

A tactical approach to nine typical holes for three golfers of different abilities. Very good as far as it goes, but finishing positions of shots are exact points. I would like to have seen target points and areas both for landing and finishing.

Harvey Penick. *Harvey Penick's Little Red Golf Book* 1992 Collins Willow. Lessons and Teaching from a Lifetime in Golf. Written from a huge amount of experience with top golfers on a large number of topics.

Dr Bob Rotella. *Golf is Not a Game of Perfect* 1995 Simon and Schuster. Excellent on mental attitudes. Dr Rotella works in America with a lot of top players. He has written other fine books in similar vein.

Tiger Woods. *How I Play Golf* 2001 Little, Brown. This is a true instruction manual, covering the whole game. The title shows that the book tells you how **he** plays, which may be slightly different from some readers! But the wisdom can be adapted if necessary to most people's games.

There now follow five authors with six books which are **essentially historical, not technical.**

Peter Alliss. *The Open* 1984 Collins. Covers the history of The Championship eloquently and in detail, with much perspective, from 1946 to 1983. One of many books that Peter Alliss has written.

Malcolm Campbell. *The Encyclopedia of Golf* 1991 Dorling Kindersley – A definitive guide to the game: its courses, characters and traditions. 1991. Outstanding sections on "The Early Game" – its origins and development to the time of writing, and much more.

John Feinstein. *The Majors* – In pursuit of Golf's

11

Holy Grail 1999 Little Brown. A brilliantly written account of the four Majors of 1998. It evocatively captures the very different natures and atmospheres at the four events. Things change all the time, but this will make a good read indefinitely.

Mark Frost

1. *The Greatest Game Ever Played* 2002 Sphere. It describes the pivotal US Open of 1913, when the unknown young amateur Francis Ouimet, a home-grown American, shocked the golf world by beating the great Harry Vardon, causing American golf to take off on the world scene. Brilliantly crafted, it covers both Vardon's and Ouimet's life stories, and the birth of modern golf, and golf history from the 1890s to WW1.

2. *The Grand Slam* 2004 Time Warner. The career of the immortal Bobby Jones, and a highly readable golf history of the period from after 1910 to 1930.

Ian T Henderson and David I Stirk. *The Compleat Golfer* 1982 Gollancz. A handy sized "illustrated history of the Royal and Ancient Game". For history, an alternative to the history section of *The Encyclopedia of Golf* above, with many good photos.

Chapter 3

Seventeen common conceptions questioned

Golf techniques, equipment and theories advance quicker all the time. Inevitably some earlier ideas stick around with many g0lfers long after the latest knowledge has overtaken them. Swing analysis by very high-speed digital cameras, giving not just many thousands, but now many millions of pictures per second is a recent development, and has yet to reach its full potential in unravelling what really happens during the swing and contact with the ball. On the one hand there is the latest conventional wisdom, as known and dispensed by the great teachers and club pros. On the other hand there are popular beliefs of what is the conventional wisdom, and these can often lag behind by a fair margin. One of the main thrusts of this book is to examine and challenge or partially question these popular beliefs, and to discuss why in my opinion they are wrong, not wholly right, or not the whole story. In no particular order:

CC1 Common Conceptions questioned (CC 1) "Golf is difficult"

Most people think it is hard to excel at golf, and it is. Hitting a small ball with a smallish clubhead is not easy. But although golf is complex, the many difficulties can be put in perspective, and at worst understood better, and reduced. Looking at the four main parts of the game:

CC1.1 Long game

Problems are that long shots involve many different movements which have to combine in the right order, and with good rhythm and timing – Chapter 8 "Long Game". When done well, as with most games and sports, it looks easy. Many golfers do not have this natural rhythm. But that is not to say that a less gainly swing, if it is reasonably consistent, cannot produce good results.

Long shots are less hard because you should know what club to take, and you don't have to work out how hard to hit it. For many long shots you are hitting to a reasonably generous target area, so the margins are often not very tight. Provided you don't go for "heroic" shots, where the margins are small, and the consequences of failure are serious, you should not be under too much pressure.

CC1.2 Pitches

These are often part-strength wedges – see Chapter 7 – "Pitching". It **is** hard to judge how hard to hit a part-strength wedge by eye, or even by yardage if done entirely by feel. unless you use a system of distance control such as described there.

But if you do use that Pelz system, and you do the groundwork, and build confidence in it, it should make this part of your game relatively easy, and one of your strengths.

CC1.3 Chipping

This really is the hardest part of golf, because as shown in Chapter 6 – "Chipping", from around the green from any particular spot you may have to decide between a wide choice of chipping methods and/or clubs to play. Not only that, but you must judge how hard to hit it – not nearly as easy as with a full shot.

But there is help at hand for all these problems in Chapter 6. If you can adopt these solutions, and then build confidence in them, the important chip shots can became a strength rather than a weakness.

CC1.4 Putting

Bad putters have problems: common ones are described in 4.3 of Chapter 5 – "Putting". Bad putters can lose at least 10 strokes or more per round compared with good putters.

But with better understanding and technique, radical improvements can be made. Putting should be one of the easiest parts of the game: no strength is needed; you know which club to take; no calculations are needed for flight paths and landing effects. A sound technique should produce good distance and direction control.

CC 2 "There is one golf swing"

This was the conventional wisdom until roughly the 1960s, before which many pros taught that the smaller shots, right down to the short putt were smaller versions of the full swing. Old films up to the early 60s show that most pros used their wrists when putting, even on short putts, and chips too. I believe the reasons were largely precedent, but also because greens were generally a little slower then: if you look at the roll-out of the putts in films of that era, they seemed to slow down quicker. Therefore they had to be hit with a little more force – hence the wrists. This probably caused a little more back-spin, which further slows the roll.

Today virtually all teachers accept that there are four main golf swings, all considerably different. I have placed them strongest swing first, but for learning golf they should be mastered the other way round – see CC 9, "Teach the full shot first".

CC2.1   Power swings

which are full swings with full coiling and uncoiling of the upper torso, and all the other components described in Chapter 8 – "The Long Game". At the top of the backswing there is a forward movement of the weight and hips, which gets you into a "pulling" position and initiates the downswing. Woods, Utilities and irons will often use the power swing.

CC2.2   Finesse swings

which use less upper torso coil, for more consistent striking and accuracy in both distance and direction. They may be used for many full shots, except when maximum carry is needed, in which case the power swing can give very roughly 10% more carry. Finesse swings are highly desirable for part-strength wedges and smaller pitches, and are dealt with in Chapter 7 – "Pitching".

CC2.3   Chips

I define a chip as a shortish shot with no wrist or

hand action. The only power comes from arm swing plus some leg action in most cases. The many possible chipping actions are very fully detailed in Chapter 6 – "Chipping".

CC2.4 Putts

The basic method accepted by Dave Pelz and most top pros today for most putts up to about 40 or 50 feet eliminates all hand, wrist and body movement except rocking of the shoulders, which moves only the arms. Over about 45 ft Pelz recommends the "chip-putt", which is more like a chip, having a little leg movement, which gives not only a little extra power, but more distance control normally. A third method which I favour for putts from the apron or fairway is the "top-spin" putt, also like the chipping action; details in Chapter 5 – "Putting".

CC 3 "Keep your left arm straight"

It is not always easy to tell exactly from photos and films whether the left arm is dead straight, or what the angle of bend of the left elbow is at the top of the backswing. Golf photography in future should involve more standardization of camera positions, and marking up of key body areas to see exactly what is happening, and to make more meaningful comparisons.

The correctness of this dictum is debatable: there are good reasons for and against a straight left arm. Possible reasons for are:

1. It promotes a wider arc, which is better than a narrower arc, because the ball is struck with less of a descending blow, which loses power.
2. A wider arc gives you more to throw at the ball

17

from further away, increasing power.

3. If your left arm is straight, it may be easier to come back to the ball with a little more precision than with a straightening arm.

Possible reasons against are:

1. A straight left arm is on its own a very weak way to propel a club – think of the squash backhand hit when the ball is a little off the floor in a plane very similar to the golf swing: much "snap" is provided by the severe bend at the elbow (roughly 90 degrees) unwinding in the downswing. As in golf a great deal of the swish comes from the wrist and hand. But in golf the left arm is braced and strengthened by the usually stronger right arm. Some of the latest breed of young professionals, who are fitter and stronger than their predecessors, probably do keep their left arm straight, or almost straight.

2. Very few of the world's top pros of very recent times actually do it! Look closely at any instruction book, as clothes often camouflage the true angles of the arm at and near the top of the backswing, and you will see that there is nearly always at least a very slight bend at the elbow there. A fine example is David Leadbetter's book *Lessons from the Golf Greats*, 1995. This shows twenty-six top pros, including two ladies, at the top with at least some bend at their left elbow, with just a single exception. This is Ernie Els, who is strong enough to keep dead straight! Ben Hogan was not far off straight, but in his classic book *The Modern Fundamentals of Golf* 1957 he shows his left arm not straight.

Summing up, the straight left arm is not the most powerful way to hit the ball, but power gained from a bent elbow might be reduced or lost through a steeper arc. If you are strong, young and flexible, the straight left arm is worth considering. If you are older, less strong and lithe, don't worry about a small amount of bend. Up to the 1890s, when the "Old St Andrew's Swing" was gradually replaced by the "modern swing" as perfected by Harry Vardon, the left elbow was typically bent a full 90 degrees or so. Bobby Jones had a good answer: in his "Tru-Vue" 3-D instructional series of 1934, he has his left arm slightly bent at the first position at the top, but while still at the top, as he moves his weight forwards, he simultaneously straightens his left arm. Did anyone swing the club better?

A special case is the one-armed golfer swinging, say, right-handed with the left arm. This action is not unlike the two-armed right-hander's swing, but without the benefit of the bracing and strengthening right arm. *The Search for the Perfect Swing* 1968 has a section devoted to left-armed only golfers with right-handed swings, by way of illustrating one example of what they call the "model left arm two-lever swing". This swing, simplified for the purposes of scientific analysis, represents a two-armed golfer who swings with a straight left arm. The book shows swing sequences for "probably the two best one-armed golfers in Britain", Alec Willmott, 8 handicap in 1968, and Bob Reid, 4 handicap. Each of them won the World One-Armed Golf Championship several times. Willmott allowed his arm to bend by up to 30 degrees at his elbow, which was necessary to obtain more power. Reid had an almost straight left arm, which he could manage because he was very strong. I am fortunate to know Nick Champness at my club, Royal Ashdown Forest GC, who is the current and seven times World One-Armed Golf Champion. He tells me that he knows both the former champions, and that Willmott with his bent left arm is less straight than Reid (now Sir Bob), who hits it a shade on the shorter side, but very straight. Nick himself thinks he bends his elbow to a degree, and he is known as a long hitter in anybody's language, but not always in the middle of the fairway! Figs 3.3 (1) and (2) are action shots of Nick taking a practice swing, and confirm that his left arm is somewhat bent, and they also show his excellent position at the initial top, and his superb finish position. These anecdotes support my theory.

CC 4 "Clubhead speed alone determines distance"

This view is unambiguously stated in *The Search for the Perfect Swing* 1968 (I call it "SPS"), which reached this conclusion based on their generally excellent and ground-breaking research in the mid-1960s. SPS adheres to that view today in a reprint in 2005.

I believe that SPS looked only at a teed-up driver or wood shot, and that their dictum may have some truth, but that it would benefit from being qualified, because I feel it is not quite the whole story, and appears to diminish the importance of the swing after impact. The two maxims CC 4 and CC 5 are very closely linked, and somewhat inseparable as discussed in the Appendix.

SPS 1968 and 2005 is such a well-respected authority on the technicalities of golf, and remains on the Preferred Reading List of both the PGA and the US PGA: accordingly many readers accept all or most of their conclusions.

SPS effectively defines clubhead speed as the speed at initial impact. They say that whatever happens after that initial impact is immaterial. The reason for this, they say, is that the driver's clubhead behaves as if it were not connected to the shaft, because it is rather "whippy", so that the golfer could not inject extra power even if he wanted to. I doubt whether this is wholly true. I believe that it is better – maybe only slightly better – to feed in more power and "drive" both during and beyond impact, rather than merely to try to "freewheel" through impact. However, I believe that most authorities, not excluding the scientists themselves, would accept that one's highest clubhead speeds cannot be attained unless one's follow-through is "good", which probably means relatively forceful and at least fairly full. I believe it is difficult to achieve maximum clubhead speed at first impact with a restricted length or powerless follow-through.

There is a second case which SPS have not written about: the shot which meets with extra resistance – typically the iron shot which takes a divot as it cuts into tough grass or turf, and uses up more of the club's energy. Irons usually have considerably stiffer shafts than drivers, and so I can hardly imagine that the iron clubhead behaves as if it were "connected by string" to the shaft. The greater stiffness of the shaft and the extra resistance of the turf suggest to me that extra drive during impact will have a beneficial effect on the distance (and accuracy) of the shot.

Of course there are many other factors at work, some much more significant to the outcome, namely degree of off-centre strike, clubhead path; launch angle and spin. These factors are often a lot more important than variations in the drive pattern through the ball, which latter has had less research put into it. The question of testing performances of irons with varying turf resistance is more complex and does not so easily lend itself to research.

I have long felt that the most effective swing both for distance and accuracy was one in which there is plenty of speed, but not so much that the clubhead is starting to lose power at around first impact: better to keep applying pressure to the ball to help overcome the ball's inertia, and any extra resistance from the turf. The evidence in favour is largely anecdotal. Many good golfers believe it is better to apply power through and beyond the ball. Nearly all top golfers continue to a full and positive finish. Top pros appear to have a wide range of swing speeds: the apparently quick swings do not appear to hit the ball noticeably further than the apparently slow swingers. (But what appears to be slow impact speed is not necessarily quite as slow as one might think.) Ernie Els appears to be very easy, with apparently moderate clubhead speed, but he hits it as far as most. Tony Jacklin was reported as saying after he won The Open in 1969 "…. The slower I swung, the farther the ball would go" (p. 53 *The Golf swing of the future* by Mindy Blake 1972). Tiger Woods is reported recently to be swinging considerably faster, but I do not think it is going further, or straighter. Els went through a period in about 2005 when he started to swing faster: I believe it improved neither his length nor accuracy. I think this debate will be proved one day, as suggested in the Appendix.

The practice swing

The main difference between the actual swing and the practice swing is that the clubhead is considerably slowed during impact with the ball. But although it is not slowed down in the practice swing, I believe one should be **trying** for identical rhythms in both swings. In the practice swing I believe the fastest speed should come just after the point of impact, which would mean it was accelerating through the ball, and would produce the loudest "swish" at that point. To achieve this one must keep "leaning on" the club until well beyond the impact area. Acceleration is an increase in speed: it is easier to get more acceleration if the clubhead is not moving absolutely flat out at impact. The most powerful swing will go from fast to even faster, but there are only a few players – strong and having good timing – who can achieve it. From medium to faster is a more sensible aim for most of us. I believe that acceleration through impact is important in order to counter the loss of energy caused by the collision and any turf resistance. My views conflict with SPS in the case of the teed driver.

All the above remarks re CC 4 apply also in essence to CC 5 below. I have explained my views on both CC 4 and CC 5 in greater detail in the Appendix for more technically-minded readers.

CC 5 "After impact nothing can alter the outcome"

This maxim is true in that the ball knows only what happens to it during the very short contact phase of half a thousandth of a second, during less than an inch of travel in contact with the clubface. But as with CC 4, it is not the whole story. Not only that, I believe it gives out an inappropriate message. Most of what I have written in CC 4 above applies equally here to CC 5, and I will not repeat it. I believe it is important to have driving force into and beyond the ball, as well as sheer speed, speed being the main influence. I explain in the Appendix how this debate may be proved one day, and why it has not been the subject of more research.

Whilst accepting that speed at impact is the main factor, I believe that speed cannot be got unless the follow-through is strong. After much thought and discussion with a leading club manufacturer (see Appendix) and other experts who should know, I still feel that positive pressure through the ball is important.

In just about every ball game the follow-through is important. The top tennis players knocking up at Wimbledon keep stroking through their ground strokes long after the ball has left their racket, and faster in the match, to give longer contact with the strings, which puts more "weight" or power into the stroke, as well as accuracy. Why do they do so if it is not necessary? The same applies to top golfers: why do they bother to complete the swing? You will see Phil Mickelson and Tiger Woods, two of the longest hitters, actually recoil or come back from the end of their follow-through when driving for maximum distance. I believe they do so in order to get the maximum possible force into their entire follow-through, because by recoiling, force is still being applied at the fullest point of the follow-through. But if they came to a stop at the fullest extension, they would have decelerated more and sooner, thus allowing less power into the follow-through. Snooker is different but similar: to get the required heavy spins on the cue ball, it has to be struck with precisely the right length and rhythm of follow-through to produce the desired effect.

There is one exception. If you have a heavy tree root, large stone, or exceptionally thick woody heather branch just beyond the ball, the last thing you want is a powerful and full follow-through – if you are gripping strongly and stiffly, you are likely to damage your hands or wrists. You should come into the ball with speed, but take care to let your wrists go as loose as possible just before impact.

I believe that the most important part of just about all golf shots is the follow-through. What happens before impact – stance, address, backswing and downswing etc. – are all very important. But all this good work can easily be spoiled if the follow-through is not good and positive. Conversely you can often get away with less than perfection up to impact if your follow-through is excellent!

CC 6 "Keep your head down"

(See also CC 7 "Keep your eye on the ball") This is right in principle, but needs elaborating. All golf swings rotate about a hub, somewhere in the chest, except that the hub moves first back, and then forward, particularly in the power swing. At address the hub is in the forward position, which should be similar, but not identical to your impact position. At the top of the backswing and before your forward weight transfer, your hub has moved back, before moving forward into your "pulling" position. The whole point of "head down" is that the (forward) hub needs to be stable, so that the clubhead returns to the right position relative to the ball, so that it can be struck in the middle of the club face for consistent contact. The reason for "keeping your head down" is so that you do not jerk your hub out of position with your head during the vital parts of the swing too soon after impact.

The main danger is lifting your head too soon, resulting in a thinned or topped shot. The ideal is to keep your head looking down at where the ball was until the point where your right arm or clubshaft reach about the horizontal on the through swing, as in Fig 3.6 – (1), which shows the head well down with the club shaft past the horizontal. From there the head **should** come up gradually, so that by the end of the swing not only has it turned to align roughly with your chest, but also it has risen up to look squarely at the ball's flight – not too soon, but just right. If you don't do this, but try to keep your head and face rigidly down for too long, your shot will suffer, because it will be harder to make a full and proper finish.

There is another aspect which affects some golfers, and I have suffered from this for 70 years. With poor posture one is inclined to sink one's head too low onto the chest both at address and throughout the swing. This restricts the turn in the backswing, because your left shoulder cannot rotate under your chin. My recommendation is to take your stance and address with your face and eyes pointing not at the ball, but at an imaginary point at least ten feet beyond the ball. Then drop your eyes without moving your head. This will keep your head up and give you freedom to make a good turn, while your eyes are looking down at the ball. Figs 3.6 – (2) and (3) show the head in the right and the wrong position.

Yet another psychological problem is that some people equate "head down" with "getting down to it". Getting down to it implies that you are really trying, and not being lazy! But if you overdo this during your downswing, the result will be a heavy shot, which will cost you. So the key thought should be to keep the hub, and with it the head, at a constant height throughout the "business" part of the swing, from takeaway until halfway through the follow-through.

A significant exception to the general rule about keeping your head down is the method used to great effect by Anneka Sorenstam and David Duval. They very deliberately and smoothly raise their head and eyes as they are hitting the ball. I would think it has its advantages. First they do not have to worry about not seeing where the ball goes, which is the major reason for looking up too soon and jerkily. Second it seems easier to get a more natural and slightly more powerful swing through and beyond the ball. I am not sure to what extent they do this on their short games, and there is no reason why it should not be tried. Both were world No 1 golfers, in particular Anneka.

CC 7 "Keep your eye(s) on the ball"

Closely related to CC6 above – "Keep your head down". Again, this advice is broadly very sound. The danger is that the ball goes away, and if you have your eyes fixed rigidly on the ball, there will be a tendency to follow it as it goes off – human nature to want to know where it has gone! One way to avoid this is to look not at the ball, but at a blade of grass an inch or so behind the ball.

Of course the eyes will follow the way your head or face is pointing, as in CC6, and as described there it is necessary and correct for the head and eyes to start to follow the ball on shots with a fuller finish from about half way through the follow-through. At the top of the backswing your head will naturally rotate a little to your right, and you may see the ball with your left eye only, as your nose may be in the way of your right eye.

What you do with your eyes becomes perhaps even more important the shorter the shot you have. For full and even part-strength wedges it is recommended by D Pelz that you finish "high", with the chest and eyes looking down the target line, and the whole body raised from its slightly crouched address position. In these cases the eyes will have stayed down, roughly as in full shots until half way through the follow-through. By coming up gradually after that, you improve your chance of making positive (accelerating) contact by finishing your swing properly.

But with chips and putts there is no physical or technical need to lift your eyes or head until after the action is over. This goes right against human nature – you badly want to know where the ball has gone! Many aspects of putting and chipping are discussed more fully in chapters 5 and 6, including the vital question: what to do with your eyes? There are many different things you can do with them for putting, and also for chipping. The top pros still "come up" quite early to follow the roll of their putts, but the difference compared with the average golfer is that they don't come up by turning their shoulders round, which will pull their system off line: they swivel their neck, so that their eyes and their body stay in line. There are not that many who stay down completely on their putts for some time after the ball has left, as does Tiger Woods – a major reason for him being one of the world's very best putters. In Chapter 6 – "Chipping", I suggest that there is no reason why a similar approach is not used for chipping, which should improve results for all skill levels. I believe this is a novel idea, and may catch on if it seems to work, but it will be hard, as it is so much against human nature.

Before leaving eyes, I must touch on the effect of many prescription glasses. A little realised problem is that looking through most parts of your lenses alters your line of sight, making the hole, or a more distant target appear to be more to one side and higher or lower than it really is. This is caused by the magnification built into most glasses, and it is greatest at the edges of the lenses, reducing towards the optical centre, at which point there should be no effect. A way to counter this problem is to swivel your neck enough to look at your target through the optical centres. Another option is not to wear your glasses, but that might stop you from seeing where your ball goes! Magnification also makes the ground appear nearer, which can be a problem for some. I don't know to what extent the eyes and brain compensate for these distortions. I don't want to put people with glasses off, or to dent the sales of the industry, and I am sure there are other optometric answers to these possible problems. I believe that contact lenses do not suffer from the directional distortion effect, or if so, much less.

CC 8 "Grip light for chips and strong for power"

I am sure some golfers believe this, or at least one of the two. But they are essentially the wrong way round. For chips, as detailed in Chapter 6, a light grip is fine if the ball is sitting up on grass offering little resistance. But most lies are not as good, and call for a slightly descending strike which will be followed by some resistance from the turf, because of which you need a firm grip to be sure of sustaining a solid stroke through the ball, and not fluffing it. On the other hand maximum power for long shots is got by using a grip on the light side, not the strong side, because a firm grip limits the movement, largely cocking, of the wrists, and therefore swing length, and so loses the power potential of a lighter grip.

A word about **grip strengths**. Imagine a scale of 0 to 10 which applies only to your own strength. Think of strength "0" as being the weakest you can possibly grip a club without it falling out of your hands and fingers. Strength "10" is the strongest that **you** (not a superman) can grip it. The less resistance you expect to encounter from the turf or sand etc, the weaker your grip can be, and the more resistance, the stronger, not forgetting the buried tree-root or rock, etc, when your grip should relax at impact – otherwise you will damage your wrists.

CC 9 "Teach the full shot first"

Some pros even today start you on the full swing, but many have recognized for a long time that beginners, or golfers going back to basics, should start at the small end of the scale. Youngsters and some older beginners will want to thrash the ball on the range immediately. But this is not the best way to get the feel of what you are doing, or to build your four swings on a solid foundation. As shown in CC2, there is not one single golf swing, but at least four main swings, all considerably different. There are two reasons why it is best to start at the smallest end. First because **stage 1** – putting from shorter distances – introduces one only of the basic movements, and the subsequent stages each add more movements, and so it is like learning to walk before you learn to run. Second because the beginner or improver can much more quickly start to get the feel of what he is trying to do, and understand it too. Also he will taste true success much sooner, and can gradually build on that success. Then progress gradually to the bigger shots – **stage 2** – longer putts; **stage 3** chips; **stage 4** part-strength pitches; **stage 5** full "finesse" pitches and irons, etc; **stage 6** power shots. An excellent way into developing a good rhythmic full swing is via the part-strength wedges, which essentially use the same swing components. These wedges should get you to finish your shots in the right position, similar to the finish on some full iron shots, as in Figs 7.3 (5) and (6).

CC 10 "Assess your hole strategy from the tee"

This maxim will have to work on many of the "away" courses you play, as you won't have a chance to do anything else. Buying a Course Planner should help you work out how to play a hole you haven't seen before. But ideally you should try to think of your final approach to the green first. For your home course, or any course which you play a lot, or at which you have an important event, a better way is to walk round it, rather than play it – this is what Bernhard Langer and some top pros do. To work out how to play any hole at your home course, get the positions and distances of the main features, probably from a Course Planner; then stand behind the green, and ask yourself first where the hole is likely to be cut. Then where your approach shot will ideally finish for those pin positions (e.g. a little below the hole). Then the area of fairway that is best to play the approach from. And then how best to get your drive or previous shot to the ideal area. These planning processes are described in detail in Chapter 4 – "Managing Your Game", which shows how you should try to plan ahead like a snooker professional, by thinking more than one move ahead at all times. Of course you will not always put your ball into the right area, and so will have to modify your plan as you play each hole, and hit less than perfect shots.

CC 11 "The Drive is the most important shot"

This may be true on difficult courses with tight fairways and/or serious trouble at the sides, and on other courses the approach shots may be more critical. Most golfers accept that the short game is pretty vital. The whole question of which is the most important part of the game is very debatable. But to build a score, to build confidence, and keep up morale, the most important thing is to be able to get the ball into the hole from short range. By short, I mean virtually every time from up to 3 feet, and a lot more often than not from 3 to 6 feet. Play as well as you like, but if you're not getting them in from near, it will gradually eat into your game.

You need to be rock-solid from up to 18 to 24 inches. This will come from a good technique, in which you have confidence. Even very short putts should be taken seriously: look at what happened to Hale Irwin in the Open in 1983. He walked up to brush in a putt of about one inch, and missed it altogether. He failed to make the play-off by one stroke. He won the US Open three times.

Clearly if you are driving and/or approaching badly, you are not going to give yourself much of a chance. But those are faults which can be corrected by your pro. But good chipping and putting will improve your game and well-being. When Olly won the Masters in 1999 his driving was poor. But he is a great iron player, and his short game was superb. Of course bad driving is not punished quite as heavily at Augusta as at other Major venues.

CC 12 "Hit all your long shots hard"

Many golfers think this. Younger players in particular because they may like to be one up on their playing partners by taking a 7-iron where the others took a 6 or a 5. Older players too consciously or unconsciously because they don't like to admit to getting older and shorter. This is bad course management and tactics, because these intermediate clubs, between the driver and the putter, should be thought of not so much as power tools, but more as precision tools, intended to produce a fairly precise carry distance and then run-out. By hitting more of a "finesse" full shot, rather than a maximum power full shot, you will get more accuracy in carry distance, and also more directional accuracy. The carry will be slightly less, but that is why we have twelve other clubs to choose from – to cover more or less all the necessary carry distances. There will be times when a little extra carry is needed, and that is the time to give it the power swing. Chapters 4 – "Managing your Game" and 7 – "Pitching" and 8 – "Long Game" discuss this topic in more detail.

CC 13 "I should play to my handicap"

Essentially true, but you should be aware that your handicap is not expected to be your **average** performance, at any level. The table, Fig 3.13 shows roughly average ranges to be expected for golfers in the 6 handicap categories, but some are steadier and others more mercurial! Category 1 golfers should be the most consistent in their ranges of performance, and consistency normally reduces with increasing handicap. For example the Category 1 golfer should average 2 or 3 shots worse than his handicap, with a normal range from best to worst of around 4 strokes under handicap to 11 over. All performances must be compared with the CSS, or "Competition Scratch Score" which can adjust to conditions, rather than the simple SSS. Similar scales work for stableford competitions, which have become more common than medals, making adjustments for differences between par and SSS.

Handicap Category	Handicap range	Approx average strokes over handicap	Approx max. strokes under handicap	Approx max strokes over handicap	Approx total range worst to best
1	Plus to 5	2.5	−4	11	15
2	6 to 12	4.5	−5	15	20
3	13 to 20	6.5	−6	18	24
4	21 to 28	8.5	−7	21	28
5 Ladies only	29 to 36 Ladies only	10	−8	24	32

Fig 3.13 – Approx average strokeplay competition performances v. CSS

The moral is not to set your expectations too high, and to become too disappointed when you drop a few early on. When things are going well, by all means compare your figures with what your handicap seems to call for. But when you have started less well, set more modest targets as you go round!

CC 14 "My 7-iron usually goes about 135 yards"

This is one example for a given player with one particular club. The point is that the range of distances for carry and carry + run with any one club can vary greatly. Chapter 4 – "Managing your game" covers this in detail, discussing the vital importance of knowing how far your ball will carry after allowing for the many possible variables. Your standard 7-iron would be hit from flat ground onto more flat ground at the same height. Different slopes and altitude at take-off and landing produce different flights and "angles of attack" when the ball first bounces, and run-out distances.

But if you add in changes or extremes in other vital factors – temperature, wind speed and direction, resistance of your lie, even larger potential differences can build up. The worst conditions for length are if you are wearing heavy winter clothing, and you are not only cold, but not warmed up when playing the first hole or two, as compared with warm muscles and light summer clothing. The effect of some more extreme combinations is that your 7-iron which "normally" goes say 125 to 130 yards through the air and runs for maybe 10 yards, will go very much less than 100 yards, or with hardish fairways and downslopes it might total well over 200 yards. A high flier off a steep upslope into a fierce wind may almost fly back into your face!

Do you find that you come up short too often on all uphill approaches, despite taking more club? If the slope is uniform and steep at 7 degrees – about 1 in 8 – it effectively turns your 7-iron into a 9-iron, losing roughly 20 yards, since the loft difference per iron is 3 to 4 degrees. Also these factors further reduce your distance:

1. Ball hits ground earlier in its flight, when it has gone less far.
2. The more spin the higher ball will climb, and lose more distance.
3. A higher flying ball is competing more against gravity.
4. Run-out up slope much less.
5. Another factor to be aware of is that distances should be measured on a horizontal scale. 100 yards horizontally is different from 100 yards

up or down a slope

Conversely on a uniform downslope your 7-iron will fly much lower – more like a 5-iron, hit the ground later in its flight, but not necessarily further, but it will run a lot more.

CC 15 "I must use only my sand-wedge from bunkers, and must hit 2 to 3 inches behind ball"

Both these thoughts are essentially wrong, as I show in Chapter 7 – "Pitching", under "Greenside Bunkers". A conventional escape from a fair lie calls for a shallow divot starting some 4 or 5 inches before the ball, and totalling some 10 inches long. This is considerably more reliable and consistent, and easier to produce than the 2 or 3 inches behind the ball that many books call for – Dave Pelz has shown that in his research.

The carry distance for a sand-wedge using this action is limited even with a full swing to something like barely over 20 yards for a pro. If we are in a greenside bunker much more than about 15 yards from where we want the ball to land, we should take more club, up to about an 8-iron, to get more carry distance. Some golfers think that because they are in the sand, it must be a sand-wedge or nothing, which is wrong for longer carries. The set-up must be similar to the sand-wedge, so as to get the necessary "bounce".

CC 16 "Greens are fairly uniformly even"

Not so around the hole, but you can't see it! Not many golfers realize that there is an important area of roughly 6 feet radius all round the hole, which behaves differently from the rest of the green, and

37

affects most putts. Much of the putting action happens in this 12 foot circle around the hole, because of golfers holing out, their footprints being far more concentrated here. But when finishing and retrieving their ball from the hole, they make sure they don't step closer than roughly 6 inches from the hole. This traffic doesn't much affect the roll of the ball in the outer circle from 6 feet to 6 inches, but it does have a marked effect at the inner approximately 6 inch plus radius from the hole edge since there is a slightly raised plateau with a slightly jagged edge of this plateau, where the footprints stop. The ball has to climb up the jagged edge of this plateau some 6 inches from the hole. It will be much less affected if it is rolling faster than very slowly, when it will be much more deflected and slowed down. But if the ball is rolling a little quicker, it will carry on with less deflection, and be more likely to hold its line and go in, This is discussed in more detail in Chapter 5 – "Putting" Fig 5.6.1 (1). The remedy is to try to make your more attacking putts finish 1 to 2 feet past the hole, so that the ball is much less affected by the edge of the higher area.

CC 17 "Golf balls roll true"

This suggests that if a ball is struck by a putter with a smooth face, it will (1) set off at right angles, provided it is hit with no side spin, and the face is normal to the line of strike, and (2) it will roll true. Unfortunately neither can be relied on, For shorter putts of up to about 30 ft plus, the putter face will probably strike many putts unevenly, at one dimple more than a neighbouring dimple. This will send the ball off at a slight angle. The effect often happens even at short distances down to 3.5 ft putts on fast downhill greens, which Pelz's fig 9.10.5 shows can miss the hole even if perfectly struck. It follows that this must be a common reason for missing putts, so it is worth looking at ways to minimize the problem – see next para. The effect quickly reduces and disappears for longer putts, as the dimples are compressed more, and even out.

The **roll** is very often influenced because most balls are very slightly out of balance because their centre of gravity is not exactly in the geometric centre, due to manufacturing tolerances. This makes most balls have a "heavy" and a "light" side. Unless the heavy and light spot (which are diametrically opposite each other) are in line with the target line of putt, the ball will be pulled a little towards its heavy side – if the light and heavy spots are exactly at the side, a straight putt can miss the hole from as little as 5 feet, due to the built-in curl. These two effects are more fully dealt with in Chapter 5 – "Putting", with ways of eliminating or minimizing them.

Chapter 4

Managing your game
My four "management" elements

This chapter is crucially important. It is more about the mind than the body and techniques. It might be thought of as "Course management", but it is much more than that key aspect – it is also mind management. I believe some ideas are new, and that this analysis is different and logical. There are many good Golf Psychologists, such as Dr Bob Rotella, whose various books will give you most of my advice, and a lot more. The main elements which follow are:

1. How best you can play the golf course and each hole – in principle, and under the conditions on the day.
2. Getting a clear plan quickly and effectively of what you are trying to do on every single shot.
3. How to handle your thought processes, and keep your state of mind calm and working efficiently, particularly when disaster strikes.
4. Maintaining and improving your fitness, health and technical ability.

1 How best to play the course and each hole – in principle and in the conditions on the day

Think of all shots as one of these three:

1. Positioning. Usually drives and subsequent shots to a fairway target area. Doesn't apply on a one-

shotter par 3, which is "Approaching". Might include a recovery shot – sometimes "re-positioning"!

2. Approaching. Your shots to the green.
3. Finishing. Short-range chips and pitches after you have missed the green, and putts.

All 3 types are important. Positioning shots should be the easiest because the margin for error is greater, whereas Approaching and Finishing call for more precision.

For your main home course, and for any other courses which are important to you, you should spend time (a) weighing them up by looking at trouble, carries and good areas to aim for, and bad areas to avoid (but as you come to play a shot, you must not think about where **not** to go, but positively only where **to** go) and (b) thinking about how to play each hole in different conditions – e.g. weather and turf conditions, and pin placements. To weigh up a hole buy a "Course Planner", and maybe pace or measure any missing key distances.

Having got the layout and distances, the best way to figure out how to play the hole is to stand behind the green and ask yourself where are the typical positions for the hole to be cut. Greens are mostly either not very sloping, or sloping, and that doesn't change. What does change with weather and turf conditions is their firmness. Now think of yourself as a snooker professional. They are so good at controlling the cue ball, or laying a snooker, that they have to think at least one or two, and sometimes several moves ahead, especially for "break building". You too can and should think ahead. Start by asking yourself where for a given pin position your approach should ideally finish. On a flattish green this might be in the hole! But on a sloping green it will usually be somewhere below the hole. The target may be an exact spot, or a small area. If the pin placement is tight, you may have to aim to finish close to the centre of the green. I have discussed these ideas with Willie Thorne, the greatest big-break builder of all time, who is credited with the most maximum 147 breaks. He has to think far ahead for a 147. His views are particularly valuable because he is also a 9-handicap golfer. Willie Thorne has kindly said that he finds my thinking useful, and agrees with it.

Next think about the ideal area from which to hit the approach, which may vary with different pin positions. The ideal approach zone may not be the easiest area to which to hit the previous shot, so you might have to compromise between the two. And so on, back to the tee shot. This will raise the key question of whether on the day the hole should be played as a one-shotter, 2-shotter, or 3 or sometimes 4-shotter. Depending on the risk/reward ratios for each shot, it may be more sensible to play e.g. a longer par 4 as a 3-shotter in slower conditions, or even in running conditions. If you settle for a conservative strategy on the day, you may find that your drive or second shot is put under much less pressure, and so can be hit less hard and with more control, and is far less likely to wind up in trouble that may be serious, which could badly increase your score. For your drives to fairways, and any further shots to fairway positions, you are trying to make the ball finish in the middle of a carefully worked-out area, which avoids danger or hazards.

But just because you plan to finish in an area, do not make the mistake of taking only general aim: always take precise aim for a particular exact point within that area.

By contrast, your approach shots are designed to land on a particular point, or smaller area, either on the green, if receptive, or short of the green, and then run onto the selected finishing target point or area on the green, e.g. below the hole on a sloping green.

2 Getting a clear plan quickly and effectively of what you are trying to do on every single shot

This heading is fairly synonymous with the so-called *pre-shot routine,* which should always involve weighing up every shot. It also can and should include preparing for the shot by e.g. visualizing it, and making one or more practice swings. The pre-shot routine should not be confused with the **pre-shot ritual.** This can and should be a vital part of the process, the routine as you consider your options, and the ritual immediately before and during your swing. The pre-shot ritual is about "training your subconscious to perform at the proper rhythm (at all times) and when you are scared". I have used some of Dave Pelz's words. A fuller description of each appears in 12.7 of his *Short Game Bible* – Secret No. 5: "The Secret of the Preshot Routine and Ritual".

There is usually a lot to be thought of before you play each shot. It is easy sometimes to forget an important element, such as the wind on a little pitch or chip. Start the thought process as early as you can, if possible well before you get to your ball. The first thought might often be to ask yourself whether your next shot should be attacking, defensive or positional. This will depend on how your competition is going, or the state of your match. It is then vital to have a very clear idea of what you are going to do on every single shot you play: if you do so, it will give you a much better chance of playing a good one. If you don't, your shot will often be spoiled, largely by indecision, but also by failure to think it out properly.

Here is a concept which I haven't come across, but I daresay may not be novel. Golfers have been doing it instinctively and/or thoughtfully as long as the game has been played. Think of yourself as the pilot of a plane. For every shot that leaves the ground, think of making a *Flight Plan*. The only shots for which this does not apply are putt-type shots, which never leave the ground – planning for these is found in Chapter 5 "Putting". Your *Flight Plan* will be in four parts. You need to think about all four of them more or less simultaneously, as they all interact. They are:

2.1 Conditions at take-off

These include the lie, texture, grain and resistance of grass and root structure or sand, slopes at ball lie and for stance, height of tee-peg if used. Some of these can be thought about before you reach the ball, but you usually can't weigh up the lie until you get there. Resistance of the turf or sand is important because driving the clubhead into it takes away some of the energy during impact, and will reduce the carry. Iron shots which take divots have to be played farther back in the stance than a ball sitting

44

up on a lush grassy lie. The easy ball sitting up will carry further than the ball struck with a slightly descending blow followed by a divot for two reasons: (1) less resistance and (2) club has nearer normal loft. Some root structures will grab the club more than others. Seaside sandy soils require accurate striking, and usually produce less carry and lower flights.

2.2 Conditions during flight

Work out exactly where you plan to make first landfall: this should preferably be a precise spot often within a target area. The target area will be larger for a shot to a fairway than for an approach shot to a green. At the same time you will be thinking about flight conditions – wind strength(s) and direction(s) along flight path, temperature, flight shape and trajectory, in relation to carry distances for the appropriate club. Your carry distances and flight trajectories may be greatly affected by possible up and down slopes at take-off, and by the height difference between take-off and landing – see Chapter 3 – Common Conception questioned 14 – "I hit my 7-iron 130 yards".

2.3 Conditions at first landfall

The key calculations here are all important, namely slopes at target landing area together with projected landfall angle, hardness or softness of ground at landfall, grass length. As Dave Pelz shows (his Figs 7.8.1 to 7.8.4 in his *Short Game Bible*), variations in the slope angle at landfall are effectively doubled for the angle of the first bounce. This has disproportionate effects on the run-out distances because of the angle of the first bounce – we know this, but don't always remember.

2.4 Conditions for run-out

Slopes in target run-out zone, turf speed (grain, length, wetness, etc), wind direction and strength there. Remember that a ball may plug if ground very soft, or run back towards you if the slope is greater than the angle of attack, or if it starts to roll back down the slope.

All of this sounds desperately over-thorough and can be slow. It should all be done, and none of it missed out, but done quickly – it speeds up play, and improves your results if you get on with it! There are perhaps three main elements to *slow play*: (1) moving slowly and inefficiently (2) thinking and deciding too slowly, and (3) taking too long over the shot. These should all be quick.

3 How to handle your thought processes, and keep your state of mind calm and working efficiently, particularly when disaster strikes

There is much excellent golf psychology in many books, e.g. by Dr Bob Rotella. Here are a few of my ideas, which should take you quite a long way. First a simple outlook:

If you play a shot well, and it gets a good result, you will naturally be pleased.

If you play a shot well, and it has an unlucky break, you played it as you meant to: be happy!

If you play a shot badly, and it has a lucky break, be happy – you got away with it!

If you play a shot badly and the result is bad, don't be unhappy – you got what you deserved.

From just about any angle it is important to enjoy your golf. Think of yourself as a lucky golfer, even if you aren't! It usually produces a better result and, far more worthwhile, it makes you a nicer person to play with or against. A main purpose is to try to keep your brain working close to peak performance even when it gets under severe stress from setbacks and disappointments. This applies not only to golf, but to most aspects of life. "Stay calm in a crisis": you are far more likely to perform better and to make good decisions if you can.

A golfing example: you are going very well in an important medal or stableford, with every chance of getting your name on a major club trophy board, when at the 17th you hook one into a terrible spot which calls for a tricky decision: what to do next? Your mind is scrambled, and you can't think clearly. But if you could be fairly calmly in control of your emotions, the chances are that you might still pull it off, or salvage a play-off or second place or whatever. But if you let go, you have little chance.

Such a disaster or impending disaster seems ghastly to the golfer at the time. The first thing to do is to put it into perspective. If you fail to win, will you be shunned by your friends or expelled from the club? Ask yourself what is the worst that could happen? Similar thought processes can work well when something goes badly wrong in everyday life – you may be seriously late for a vital appointment, and blaming yourself or factors beyond your control. A most handy reaction is to try to see the funny side of a desperate situation *even as it is happening*! Not easily done, but it can keep you sane and rational.

Most of us want to give a good account of ourselves on the golf course. If we play badly, we feel we are letting not only ourselves down, but also our playing companions. But have you thought that in a medal or stableford, the worse the score you return, the more of your fellow-competitors you will make happy? Of course we all want to do well, and win matches and events when we can. Look for "something to take away" from every round of golf. If you have played badly, you can identify some of your important faults – go to your pro to sort them out.

If you have just played a bad shot, you will naturally be disappointed, and maybe upset. I recommend you immediately say something like "Dammit, you idiot!" – nothing too strong or that might offend anyone, or damage the golf course or your club. But after thinking for just a moment what you did wrong, and maybe rehearsing your swing, immediately wipe your mind clear, with, say, a little shake of the head, maybe with your eyes closed! Then you are immediately back to normal – the slate is clear. You shouldn't be very upset, because whatever level of skill you inhabit, you are bound to play at least a few bad shots. The world's best don't let themselves be put off by a bad shot – often the reverse.

We want to do well and win the match or event. Obviously determination is important. But perhaps even more so is to keep up our belief that it will happen. If we truly believe it will, it probably will. Here I must distinguish between winning and playing well. The true lover of the game would rather play well and lose, than win, playing badly. Similarly, would you rather hit a putt well, and it unluckily just stayed out, or hit a less good putt, which luckily went in? Surely we are trying to do both – play well and win. Both are important to us.

We need to (1) know how to play all or most of the shots, and (2) when to play which type of shot (near the green there can be at least two different ways), and (3) be able to do so under pressure – easier said than done!

Mental strength and steadiness need to be accompanied by the resolve to execute correctly what we know we have to do: this is far more likely to happen if we can control our minds in these sorts of ways.

4 Maintaining and improving your fitness, health and technical ability

These aims are too obvious to be written down. Fitness includes strength, flexibility and endurance. But they are part of the process of "Managing your game". They are longer-term goals, which need to be worked at if we are to improve these things, and with them our golf and probably our enjoyment. Getting better at golf is a good challenge for most people, and they would see it as a worthwhile aim. It can be both a worthwhile physical and intellectual challenge.

Chapter 5

Putting

1 Putting is vital: you can putt well.

Putting: possibly the most important part of golf. There are three main parts to golf: (1) Positioning, (2) Approaching, and (3) Finishing. Putting is usually much the largest part of Finishing. The difference between putting well and putting badly can be well over ten strokes a round. Of course even more strokes can be lost by bad Positioning and/or bad Approaching. Errors on longer shots will be due to weaknesses in technique and in "Managing Your Game" – Chapter 4. But there is one crucial difference between the longer Positioning and Approaching shots and the Finishing shots. That is that most of us will never be able to hit the long shots as far and as accurately as the top golfers. But when it comes to Finishing, there is no reason why many golfers, however old, handicapped or weak, should not be able to putt and play the little shots around the green a lot better than they do now, and almost as well as the top players. This because physical strength is hardly a factor.

As I have said in other chapters, *Dave Pelz's Putting Bible* 2000 gives a masterly review in nearly 400 pages of the vast amount of research he has done, and sets out the many things we can do to improve our putting radically. I strongly recommend that book, and I agree with all he says about putting on the greens. As elsewhere in my book, I have come up with several new ideas of my own, but I have invoked Pelz to fill the many gaps which I have deliberately left.

Putting is a lot easier than chipping, because you know which club and what action you will use; it is 2-dimensional as the ball never leaves the ground, and so you don't have to worry about trajectories and run-outs.

2   Putting actions for different putt lengths

2.1   "Standard" putting action up to about 45 feet

Until the 1960s and 70s, top players used a huge variety of different actions or styles. Today most pros use an essentially similar action. But they use many variations in grips. Pelz has written outstandingly the best book I know of on putting. I can summarise his main recommendations on the basic action, which generally apply to all putts up to about 45 feet. Pelz says stand with your feet hips and shoulders square to and "parallel left" of the aim line. Position your eyes in a plane vertically above the ball, preferably behind the ball, with the ball a little forward in the stance. Grip lightly, and swing with the arms and shoulders only rocking and no wrist or hand action, and stroke the ball squarely in the middle of the putter blade.

2.2 "Chip-putt" action for longer putts

Pelz recommends his standard action up to about 45 feet, and I agree. Over ca. 45 ft he recommends a "chip-putt" action, which is similar to the basic chipping action, i.e. totally wristless and lacking hand action, but it adds a small amount of leg movement, as in Chapter 6 – "Chipping". This gives a little more power, which is valuable for long putts. At a certain distance or putt strength the chip-putt starts to give you better distance control than the conventional putt, and distance control is more important on longer putts: you should experiment to see what your break-even distance is. But directional control need not be worse with the chip-putt. Also the chip-putt starts to feel more natural at the longer distances. As with the chip, try to keep your putter head from "overtaking" your hands.

2.3 Putting from off the green

If you are off the green and the apron or fairway look to give a reliable roll, putting it can be the percentage shot, rather than a chip or little pitch, particularly e.g. on a seaside course with fast sloping greens and winds. Pelz does not suggest any change from the chip-putt when putting from distances over about 45 feet from the apron (or smooth fairway). I differ. This is the one and only point on which I disagree with anything that Pelz says in his 800+ pages of *Putting* and *Short Game* "Bibles". I believe that the standard chip-putt promotes more sliding and less early rolling from off the green. Better is a more top-spinning action, which I find gives superior distance control. This is hard to prove. The reason, if it is true, is that a normal action involves more variability in the drag on the ball, and therefore in the energy remaining with the ball after it starts truly to roll. I find it works, provided it is done with conviction. Please give it a serious try!

Don't ever putt from the rough, unless the grass is short, and the grain is with you!

2.4 Other putting actions

Some authorities including Mindy Blake in his two books (*see* Bibliography) favours a top-spinning stroke, which brushes up over the ball with a slightly delofted or even closed putter blade, striking the ball at, or a little above its centre. There are a huge number of variations in putting actions, grips etc. It may make sense to have in addition to your standard action and set-up for short and medium length putts, a second-favourite method to fall back on if the first one isn't succeeding on the day. I have sometimes putted so badly that I could do better on short putts with a 2-iron or even a "bellied" wedge!

3   Some important choices

There are many possible variables. Three of the most important are:

3.1   Rhythm and Tempo

Pelz says the swing should be very much like a pendulum, with virtually no driving force through the ball, other than the weight of the putter. Pelz accepts that a small degree of acceleration is needed for the best results, which is achieved, because the fastest part of the swing occurs just after impact, and the follow-through is slightly longer than the backswing. There is a lot involved, and for detailed explanations of all the many factors in putting, there is no substitute to reading the book *Dave Pelz's Putting Bible.*

If the various driving muscles are taken out of the

equation, which they should be, you should not succumb to sudden surges of power under pressure. It is then purely the length of the backswing (and the slightly longer follow-through) that controls the strength of the putt.

In addition I strongly recommend a slight pause at the top of the backswing, to avoid possible snatching and timing errors. This pause gives you a moment to be sure that you have gone back as far as you intended.

Tempo is the speed of the swing: I believe an even tempo is desirable, which means that the swing should take the same time for all swing lengths. Swing to a count of "one – two" or "one – pause – two". This will produce the slowest putterhead speeds for the shortest swings, and vice-versa. Having decided how long a swing to make, **trust** your judgement: be sure to give your putts the length and standard tempo of swing on which you have decided.

3.2 Grips and grip strength

Even today there are many different grips used by the pros. I won't describe them. The grip should be reasonably comfortable, and should discourage hands and wrists from supplying power or moving the putter out of line. The front-hand-low grip has the disadvantage that it feels a little unnatural, but the advantage that it makes the shoulders more level, which helps if you are older, or have a back problem, and also helps you get a good follow-through.

Grip strength should be as light as possible, so as to keep the hands and wrists out of it. On my scale of 0 to 10, which is personal to your own strength, where "0" is the lightest you can possibly grip it without it falling out of your hands, and "10" is the tightest that you can possibly grip it, I suggest you try strength "1". Normally you would want the putter sole to lie flat on the ground at its natural angle: to achieve this, you need to grip it more firmly than if it were just hanging down vertically under its own weight.

Possible exceptions to the general practice of having the sole flat include the great putter Isao Aoki, who had the heel grounded and the toe well up in the air (shades of Seve too). It seems all wrong, but the logic for it might be that the part of the putter face that strikes the ball is up in the air, and so catches the ball more than half-way up, which is a good way to get it rolling sooner.

There is a possible opposite way to produce a similar effect, namely to let the putter hang vertically, so that the toe is close to the ground, and the heel raised. This way one can get an even more truly pendulum effect, while keeping the higher impact point on the ball, as shown in Fig 5.3.2.- (1). The grip force needed to hold the putter shaft vertical is less, because no force is needed to keep the weight of the head up. However, this method may conflict with the current Rules of Golf 2008 to 2011, which state that for putters which can effectively be used in a vertical or close-to-vertical position, the shaft "may be required to diverge from vertical by up to 25 degrees". This seems to be a potential attack on the long broom-handle putters, which are debatably close to the original spirit of the game.

3.3 What to do with your eyes

You must do **something** with your eyes during and after the strike. Many top pros swivel their head quite soon after the strike, keeping their eyes in line with the putt, so that their shoulders are not turned off line by looking up the wrong way, and so pulling the putt to the left. A few top pros, notably Tiger Woods, keep from looking up at all until the ball is well on its way. Precisely what they do with their eyes may vary. There are two reasons why it is good to "stay down". First you keep a stable position throughout the stroke, including the important follow-through. Second you can concentrate better on the *feel* of the follow-through, without having the distraction of looking up to see where the ball has gone, until some time after you complete the stroke.

There are various things you can do with your eyes, and I assume you have two eyes. Possible "eye actions" include:

1   Close both eyes on impact. Excellent, because you see the ball well up to impact, and then retain stability and have better feel during the follow-through.
2   Close front eye on impact. Almost as good if disciplined and you keep back eye from seeing more than a few inches beyond ball.
3   Look at ball, and don't come up early. Needs discipline, but natural tendency to follow the ball as it goes away.
4   Look at blade of grass just behind ball. Better than 3 above, as the blade doesn't move!
5   Keep eyes closed throughout stroke. Fair, but hard to be as accurate in strike point on putter,

as you can't see what you are doing.

6 Look at hole throughout. Can work well, but problem as 5 above with accurate striking.

7 Look at some other spot throughout. Probably worst of all, as poor strike accuracy, and tendency to look up.

8 Follow putter blade with both eyes throughout stroke, and then optionally follow ball to hole.

9 Follow ball to hole from exact moment when you strike it (rather like Anneka Sorenstam's full shots).

For the first five of the above eye actions, try to keep your eye(s) closed or steady on a count of say "back – pause – through – down – open and up". The longer you can stay down on the "down" count, the better – hard to do, but rewarding. Award yourself a point for moral fibre if you succeed, even if the putt misses – but it will go in more often.

4 Weighing up your putt

You must always have a clear idea of what you plan to do with every putt, as every golf shot. The first question is how hard to hit it, which means how close it should finish, and where, should it not go in. There are several different target strengths for all putts, best defined by the distance past the hole that they would finish if they miss. The starting point for weighing a putt up is the state of your match or competition.

4.1 The five possible match/game situations

1 "Last-chance" – for a half, your match-play opponent having finished, or for one point in a sta-

bleford. Must pass the hole by at least 1 to 2 feet if missing. (You should know that Dave Pelz has found that the best chance for putts to go in is if they would have passed the hole by 17 inches.) This is because of the "lumpy doughnut" effect, explained in section 6.1 below. If from under 6 feet, usually be firm or very firm (see 5.1 below).

A 'last-chance' putt for a half or a point should always be easier to hole than an identical putt for a win or for 2 points, because you can be bolder and if you are going to miss, there is no difference between leaving it one inch short, or running it right off the green. Concessions Policy. In matchplay, as a general rule, if in doubt, it is both sensible and decent to concede a short putt if it is for a half, but to make your opponent putt if it is for a win. You might not want to win a hole through a missed very short putt, but for your opponent to win it, he should do so properly. A short putt for a win imposes extra pressure, since he could easily knock it a greater distance past, and you end up possibly winning the hole, or at worst halving it if he misses.

2. Possible win, with opponent still to putt. Tactics will depend on exact circumstances, permutations being too numerous to discuss. Might be anything from boldly attacking to "give the hole a chance, but don't 3-putt". One to two feet past will usually apply.

3. Stroke-play: strict medal, or stableford where the (first) putt is for at least 2 points. For short putts up to 6 ft. see section 5.1 below. For "holeable" putts – i.e. from up to about 20 to 25

feet, pass hole by 1 to 2 feet. For longer putts a "dead lag" or "lag plus 3 to 6 inches" is better, to avoid 3-putting.

4. Two to win in a match. Dead lag always. Dead lag means ball would stop in centre of hole if hole was not there.

5. Three to win in a match. First putt should finish dead weight and a little below hole,

4.2 Factors affecting speed and line

Obviously you should look at all the slopes, speed, grain and dampness of grass and wind effect, which is often underestimated. A good way to assess the general slopes is to start looking at them some time before you reach the green. Ideally you might look at the putt from behind the hole, noting the important slopes around the hole, and from the low side, and from behind the ball. But the first two steps around the hole take time, and should often be left out, to speed play. For speed, the key factors are height difference between your ball start position and the hole, grass speed, including grain effect, and wind. Grain may be influenced by recent rain from water run-off, recent sunlight or currently prevailing wind, and also mower grain, which is easily seen, can be a sizeable factor. For side effects that give rise to break, it is the slopes themselves, coupled with estimated roll speed at those places along the path. On wet greens breaks are reduced.

4.3 The two most common faults, and how to avoid them

The average amateur ...

1 **Underestimates the break.** The break at the hole

is a projection of the starting target line, which is usually farther out than we think. Most of us try to visualise the path of the putt, which is what we should do. However, we see the maximum apparent break some way along the path, and think that is the line, forgetting that the putt has already taken a little break before it gets to that point. If we correctly aim a little higher up the slope, we will need to strike the ball a shade harder, as it has to go a shade more uphill.

2. **Leaves it short of the hole.** For putts that are "holeable" – up to very roughly 15 to 20 feet or more – one should aim to pass the hole by the "standard" 1 to 2 feet. Putts that don't reach the hole very rarely go in!

The net effect of these two errors is that most putts miss the hole on the low side, and never have a chance of going in. For "longer" putts it usually makes more sense to play a "dead lag", where you aim to finish the ball in the exact centre of the hole, so as to avoid 3-putting. On heavily sloping greens you may need to think of leaving your approach putt below the hole.

5   Execution of putt

You have worked out exactly what line and strength you need for a particular putt and game situation. This question of many different strengths and lines applies mostly from close range up to around 6 feet. There remain two things to do:

1. Line up your putter to your selected target line. An aid to getting it right is, with your eyes over the target line, to put your putter down lightly, and to joggle it round slightly this way and that,

until you are satisfied that it is pointing the right way. Then put your hands on; then take your stance.

2. Swing your putter true along the target line, stroking the ball in the putter's affective centre .

5.1 Short breaking putts up to 6 feet

Nobody should ever miss a 12 inch putt, provided some care is taken. But very short putts down to less than one inch can be missed, or double-hit through lack of care: Hale Irwin in the 1983 Open missed his one-inch putt altogether as he was walking up to brush it in, and with it the play-off by one stroke. Up to a certain distance you should knock the putt boldy in, paying little or no attention to the lie or grain. But in the worst-case scenario, namely a quick downhill side-breaker with grain helping the ball break even more, in a medal situation, you would naturally start to get nervous from as little as 12 or 15 inches. Short putts up to 6 feet might have one of these plans, which apply to breaking putts:

Firm, to take out virtually all the break. Use this for all putts up to about 15", and for many side-sloping putts up to about 4 feet. If it misses, it will go a long way past, but if it is a "last-chance" try, it won't matter, and it will be your best chance of holing it.

Fairly firm, to take out some of the break. This will go a fair amount past if it misses, but may stand a better chance of success than the more dead-weight putt, which has to match almost perfect line with almost perfect strength.

Standard "Pelz" finish 1 to 2 feet past hole if it misses. This is the strength of strike most likely to go in, allowing for the "lumpy doughnut". It should be used if there is a risk of 3-putting.

"Dead lag plus." Would go about 3 to 6 inches past if it misses, and might be thought of as a "dead weight" putt. Some pros, including the great Bobby Jones, favoured it, as they roll past the edge slowly enough to drop in, and if they don't drop, you are left with only 3 to 6 inches. Many believe it makes the hole wider, which may be true, but much more likely to drop from the high side

"Dead Lag". Aim for the ball to die in the centre of hole. Use it when you have two for the hole.

5.2 Examples of putt paths for sharply breaking putts from 4 feet

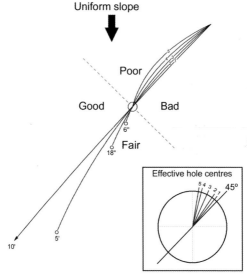

Fig 5.2 Sharply breaking 4 foot putts

The diagram Fig 5.2 shows typical paths for a fast breaking 4 foot putt at the five different speeds at which it can be played. For virtually all shorter putts up to about 15 feet, especially breaking putts, which most are, think of four quadrants, as shown. Any putt finishing short will not go in – area C, poor – short and high, and area D, bad – short and low. A missing putt finishing in area B, fair – long and low, has little chance of going in. But a missing putt finishing in area A, good – long and high, will stand some chance of going in, since a ball will drop in by gravity off the upper lip, and less so off the lower lip. Pelz found that most pros and even more amateurs underestimate the breaks, and so they miss mostly on the unsatisfactory low side. The centre of the effective front of the hole moves round from its visible centre as the putt speed reduces and the break increases. But in Fig. 5.2 you must aim wider than the apparent hole centre.

6   Three things you should perhaps know

I say "perhaps", because knowing about the last two are a mixed blessing – they might serve more to confuse and worry some people, but for others they could provide a handy excuse for a well-struck putt just missing! Not many amateurs even today know about these three factors. But you can take action to minimize their effects. They are of course all in *Dave Pelz's Putting Bible*, and touched on in Chapter 3, CCs 16 and 17. They are:

6.1   The "Lumpy doughnut"

Everyone should know about this American term, written "donut". It is a roughly circular area of

some 6 inches all around the hole, which no one
ever steps on when holing out and picking the ball
out of the hole. As a result it remains smooth and
not trodden down, even after hundreds of golfers
have been round.

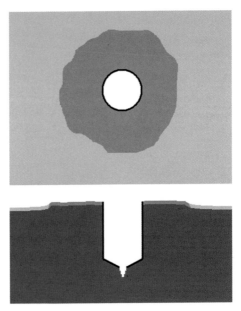

Fig 6.1 The Lumpy doughnut

Fig 6.1 shows it in plan and section through the
hole. Outside the 6 inch ring, all the ground is mod-
erately evenly trodden down, especially in the range
from 6 inches to 6 feet from the hole, where most of
the treading is. The effect is of a roughly circular
ridge surrounding a slightly higher plateau 6 inches
or so around the hole. But the edge of the ridge is
not a perfect circle – it is slightly irregular, with random footprints and spikemarks, not usually visible.
The putted ball has to climb the ridge. A ball rolling
very slowly is more easily deflected by the smallest

Fig 3.3 – (1) World One-Armed Golf Champion at top of backswing, before weight transfer. Note left arm bend. Dynamic photo from practice swing.

Fig 3.3 – (2) Champion's superb finish – from same practice swing.

Fig 3.6 – (2) Head correctly up, eyes down, to allow full shoulder turn.

Fig 3.6 – (3) Head wrongly down into chest, restricting shoulder turn.

Fig 3.6 – (1) Eyes still looking down when clubshaft halfway to finish.

Fig 5.3.2 – (1) Truly vertical pendulum putt address.

Fig 6.4.2.1 – (1) Basic square flat chip address.

Fig 6.4.2.1 – (2) Standard square flat chip address.

Fig 6.4.2.1 – (3)
Standard square flat
chip backswing.

Fig 6.4.2.1 – (4)
Standard square flat
chip finish. Note no
hand action at all.

Fig 6.4.2.2 Cut chip, flat from good lie. Feet should be closer together!

Fig 6.4.2.3 – (1) Square toed chip address. Ball should be a little nearer toes.

Fig 6.4.2.3 – (2) Toed square chip. Line to camera should be 1" more to the left of picture.

Fig 6.4.3 – (1) Putt-chip address.

Fig 7.3 – (1) 7.00 o'clock pitch, with left arm backswing 30 deg above vertical.

Fig 7.3 – (2) 8.00 o'clock pitch, left arm 60 deg above vertical.

Fig 7.3 – (3) 9.00 0'clock pitch, left arm horizontal, or 90 deg above vertical.

Fig 7.3 – (4) 10.30 o'clock pitch – left arm was meant to be at 10.00 o'clock, but has gone a shade further!

Fig 7.3 – (5) Part-strength wedge – full finish with club vertical.

Fig 7.3 – (6) Part-strength wedge full finish to horizontal.

Fig 8.3.4 – (1) Young professional at initial top of backswing, before weight transfer forward into 'pulling' position.

Fig 8.3.4 – (2) Young pro at 2nd position at top of backswing, after weight transfer.

Fig 8.3.4 – (3) As far back as 74-year old author can get at top of backswing, before weight transfer.

Fig 8.3.4 – (4) After transfer forward of hips and weight into 'pulling' position.

Fig 8.3.6.2 – (1) Wrist hinge is only movement – maximum possible 'backswing'.

Fig 8.3.6.2 – (2) Wrist hinge only – maximum possible finish.

Fig 8.3.6.3 – (1)
Forearm rotation only
movement – max.
possible backswing.

Fig 8.3.6.3 – (2)
Forearm rotation only
movement – max.
possible finish, but
arms have wrongly
moved forward too.

Fig 8.3.6.1 Wrists alone cocked, with no other movements of hands or anything else.

irregularity. But a ball with a little more pace on it when it "climbs the ridge" is less affected. The edge of the ridge with its random irregularities will easily kick a very slow moving ball a bit off line, making it finish short and/or wide. D Pelz has done huge numbers of tests, and found that the best chance of holing most putts is if the ball were to finish 17" beyond the hole, had the hole not been there! Ways to practice and simulate this effect follow in this chapter. The main lesson is: "don't be short on short and many medium putts up to around 20 feet, but try to make them pass the hole by a foot or two!

The next two things are controversial: you have to be pretty keen and a bit of an "anorak" to know about them, or bother with them. Pros know them, and top amateurs should be aware of them, so that they can take mitigating action. When you see the pros replace their ball carefully even on particularly short putts, it is to combat these next two effects.

6.2 The dimple effect

On shorter putts, up to around say 20 feet, the putter hardly compresses the ball, and so it contacts only two dimples across the ball's width. It is likely that one dimple will be contacted more than its neighbour, and that will make the ball go away slightly off square. To minimise this effect, line the ball up with the seam or "equator" along the target line, because the dimples are slightly further away from the equator. As the putt length increases, the ball becomes a little more compressed, and the dimple effect goes away. Pelz found (his Table 9.10.5) that short putts on very fast greens, being hit very softly, compress the dimples less, and can cause putts to miss. It is not easy to summarise all his work in a few words: the serious student should look up the details.

6.3 The centre of gravity is rarely in the exact middle of the ball

This seems absurd, but with manufacturing tolerances, very few balls are "perfect". Nearly all balls have a "heavy" side and a "light" side opposite it. An effective and simple way to find the exact light spot is to put a solution of Epsom salts in an open glass, strengthening it until the golf ball just floats. Add a drop of Fairy Liquid to promote free rotation, and spin the ball. You will see that it always comes to rest at the same spot – this is the light side. Take it out, dry it at that spot, and mark it indelibly. The degree of eccentricity varies from ball to ball. To see the effect, it is greatest on a fast surface. Ideal is a billiard table, which rolls at around 23 on the Stimpmeter, and **exaggerates** the effect. From one end aim a golf ball with a cue at a far corner pocket in three different ways: (1) light spot right; (2) light spot left, and (3) light spot on top. If the table is truly level, No 1 will go somewhat left, No 2 same amount right, and No 3 straight. If played softly, with just enough strength to reach the opposite far corner pocket, the amount of deviation with most golf balls will be about 3 inches each way over a distance of 10 feet. On a real green it will be considerably less, as it is much slower, at between ca. 7 to 10 on the Stimpmeter for most greens. Pelz found (his Table 9.8.4) that with a ball set up in the worst alignment, with the eccentricity at the side, the range at which it just starts to miss was 13 feet at a small CG offset of 0.002 inches down to 5 feet at a large offset in CG of 0.005 inches, all at a Stimpmeter reading of 9.5 and for straight putts.

7 Realistic expectations of success

Back in the 1970s, top American pros would hole only about 50% of putts from 6 feet, with the best putters holing 55%. Surprisingly mainly British pros at Birkdale in the 1964 British Masters had a slightly higher success rate at 6 feet according to *Search for the Perfect Swing*. With improvements in techniques and slightly smoother greens, this percentage has improved, and Tiger Woods seems to hole almost everything when in form. But they also miss occasionally from 3 feet, and because they charge it from 3 ft, it often finishes more than 3 ft away. The "average" golfer will probably do a lot worse. But from short range the firm putt is still probably the percentage choice for a curling short putt, both for the pros, and often for us.

8 Mental problems

I have dealt with many of the physical aspects of putting and with normal mental considerations in this chapter. I now touch on three more severe mental problems.

8.1 You start to miss very short "easy" putts

The hardest putts can be the easiest, because we feel we are expected to hole them, and that we would be very stupid to miss them, and so are afraid of missing. In this way one can on some days be more likely to hole a 4 to 6 foot putt than an 18 inch to 3 foot putt, because the longer putt does not carry the same fear factor. The true difficulty of putts can vary enormously, from very short, fast downhill sliders to easy longer uphill putts. To overcome this occasional problem, make sure your basics are right. On a short putt I give myself marks if I have stayed down on it and stroked it right, even if it doesn't drop! But if I do, they usually go down.

8.2 You don't know how hard to hit any putt, and you worry about it

This may be a problem if your power comes from hand or wrist action, or from forcing your arms through at variable tempo. But if you stick to the good techniques recommended, in which virtually no muscles play any part, then the chosen length of your swing should be about right for distance.

8.3 You get "the yips"

This can be a terrible problem, sometimes beyond the scope of technical solutions, unlike another damaging problem, shanking. I am lucky enough not to have had it. I have heard about it, but can't remember seeing anyone do it! In some form it has afflicted some of the very greatest players. I don't feel qualified to write about it, but I hear that much has been written.

9 Practice simulations

You can practice your putting in up to three places:

9.1 Practice putting green

Obviously most practisers putt to a hole. For short putts, it's best to choose a hole on a fair slope, and to putt all round it. Think of all missed putts as falling into one of four quadrants broadly as in Fig 5.2, which is for fast breaking 4 foot putts. For longer putts the four quadrants are very similar in principle: the best missing putts would finish long and above the hole. A fair putt would finish long and below. A poor putt would finish short and high, and a bad putt would finish short and low.

A better method for a practice green would be to find an old filled-in hole, preferably on a slight slope: putting to this should let you see (a) whether it goes in, and (b) how far past it would have rolled. There are two small problems: (1) you may be encouraged to lift your eyes and head early on the very short ones, for which it is normally better to hear them drop, not see them drop, and (2) the "lumpy doughnut" effect will not be present, unless you create it artificially by walking round and round it in a small ring roughly 6"to say 2 or 3 feet from the hole.

Another way is to find a thin, slightly flexible disc of around 4.25" diameter, using it as your hole. An example is the circular rubber jar-openers, sometimes 4.9" diameter, which are perfectly acceptable, because if a ball just catches the rim, it is turned away realistically.

Take a length of string about 10 ft long, and starting from one end mark a line with an indelible pen every 12" for 6 ft in all. These marks will represent distances of 6, 5, 4, 3, 2, 1 and 0 feet from the hole. Then make another mark 4.25" to represent the hole itself, and after that, say another 6", 18" and say 3 ft beyond the hole. This portable measuring stick can then be used either on a practice green, or indoors on a carpet, with the false hole disc. Lay the string alongside the line of the putt, so that you can easily set the ball at any chosen distance, and know immediately what that distance is, either putting to a real hole or a false hole. It may be useful to get to know the distances for short putts. They can be practiced at exact distances at 1 foot intervals from 1 ft to 6 ft. Using these exact footage distances, experiment for the different slopes and breaks with the five different strength putts, imagining different scenarios for the state of the match or competition.

9.2 Indoors

The more natural slope you can find on a suitable carpet, the better – living in an old house would help. Use the marked-up string, as before. For the firm putts put a cushion behind the end of your string. A minor problem is that it is hard to simulate the "lumpy doughnut". But if you could find a circle about 16 inches diameter of suitable thin material to represent the plateau around the hole, and set the rubber or other disc into it, the effect would be complete. Re carpet speeds, you might encounter anything between about 3 or less on the Stimpmeter up to more than 20 – the quicker the carpet the better, as it accentuates break. I believe that putting on surfaces very different from the normal range of green speeds, which is roughly 6 to 10, whether artificial or grass, does not spoil ones feel for real greens, as one immediately adapts.

9.3 Your own green

Chapters 12 (Your own Short Game course) and 13 (Golf at Home) describe ways of achieving your own green or greens, grass or artificial, which could be used for these practice exercises, and for longer putt practice. There are also various accessories available from Dave Pelz and others, such as sloped putting surfaces.

Chapter 6

Chipping

1 Chips – the hardest shots

The "chip" is probably the hardest shot in golf, because from many spots off the green you could play the ball in a bewildering variety of different ways, and only you can decide which way. They might include more than one type of chip, with a choice of clubs, sometimes a little pitch, or your putter from off the green may be the percentage shot. I suggest several chip variations, with their pros and cons. But you do not have to play all of them. A second problem is how hard to hit it? I offer two suggestions. A third problem is that chipping requires mental toughness – doing what you know is right under severe pressure and avoiding "flubbing", which is often caused by lack of firm resolve, and deceleration.

2 What is a chip?

I define a chip as having no wrist or hand action, i.e. no wrist cocking or uncocking or hingeing, or any forearm rotation, all of which makes it much simpler, and less prone to problems, including a rush of blood when under pressure. This because the movement is made by some of the larger muscles – arms, and a little leg action in many cases – whose power should be more consistent. Shorter range shots involving wrist cocking are not chips, but pitch shots, as are greenside bunker shots – see Chapter 7 – "Pitching".

3 The lies you will meet

3.1 Sitting fairly well up

If your ball is sitting up well, e.g. on a grassy tuft, you do not have to come down on it – a good way may be to sweep it from around the middle of your stance, as gauged from the middles of your ankles, and not your toes. The swept chip meets with little resistance from the grass after impact, and so can be played with a light grip, and the club delofted only a little. And there is less chance of fluffing it. With little spin applied, your ball should roll more consistently for better results than the squeezed chip from a good or less good lie.

3.2 Sitting down in the grass

You must come down on the ball with some steepness, so as to keep the amount of grass you have to cut through to a minimum. This means playing it from much more around your back foot, thus delofting the club, and taking a more lofted club to compensate. I assume there is grass under the ball as well as behind the ball. Because there is more resistance to your stroke, you must grip the club quite firmly, and be positive in your contact and follow-through, even though it is short. For these cases and the next section 3.3 the weight should be more on the front foot.

3.3 In a divot or on "hardpan"

There is no grass, only hardish earth under the ball. Again a steep angle of approach is called for, and there is little margin for error – contact must be precise, hitting the ball (on the right part of the clubface) before you hit the hard-packed earth. Again a firm grip and positive hit.

4 Chipping variables and variations in chipping actions

4.1 Chipping variables

The main variables are:

1. Loft of the club, by delofting or uplofting it; usually done by playing the ball further back or forward maybe, coupled with opening the face by pointing it to the right of target for extra loft with wedges.

2. Lie of the club. The natural lie is with the club square to target and resting naturally on the ground when the golfer is a "normal" distance from the ball. Some chipping methods involve bringing the ball much closer to the toes, making the shaft more vertical than its natural angle.

3. "Bounce" of sole. This usually applies more to sand-type wedges, which have some degree of bounce. Opening the clubface by pointing it to the right increases bounce as well as the loft, and vice-versa. In principle bounce changes can apply to any club, non-sand wedges usually having zero bounce.

4.2 Chipping actions and what to do with your eyes

These 4 chip variations all have the same basic action, as for No. 1, the standard square chip. Some are optional. Good positive (accelerating) contact is important for all chips, as for virtually all golf shots. A new idea, as far as I know, is to follow my guidance in Chapter 5 – "Putting" – section 3.3 – "What to do with your eyes", using preferably eye action No. 1 – closing both eyes on impact, for the same reasons as for putting. The chipping action is so small that it does not require any lifting of the head before completing the swing, just as in putting, but unlike fuller shots. If it were adopted by some top pros, and it proved successful, it would quickly catch on, even though it runs contrary to the human instinct of wanting to know immediately where the ball has gone! But if you train yourself to keep your eyes closed for one or two seconds after the finish, you will still see most of the action.

4.2.1 Standard square chip, sole flat

Every golfer should know how to play the standard chip. "Square" means the clubface points along the target lie, and is swung along it. The feet and body may be square or "open". Delofting depends on the lie. Take the club back with the arms only, no wrist or hand action, but adding a modest amount of leg action, which causes a little hip turn. A good way to maintain consistent the height of the hub of rotation is to make the right leg straighten by the end of the backswing, and the left leg straighten by the end. Normally addressed in centre of club, or a shade towards toe. A common error with all chips is to snatch them by being too quick. To overcome this, try consciously pausing at the end of the backswing. Can be used for any iron from about 4-iron down to all wedges, and for any distance up to a long chip. Try not to let the clubhead "overtake your hands". Figs 6.4.2.1 – (2), (3) and (4) show the address, the backswing and the finish. Fig 6.4.2.1 – (1) shows the address from behind.

Some pros. Easy lining up and good for directional accuracy. Natural. Good for any length up to long.

Some cons. From poorer lies, fluffs, thins and shanks possible; requires precise execution;. risk of double-hit for shorter chips; can put divots in your lawn!

4.2.2 Cut or open chip, sole flat

A very good one to know – fairly essential. Applies only to wedges, when more loft than standard wedge chips is needed. Works with any lie with grass under ball, but not well from divots or hardpan (3.3) because opening club increases bounce, so that you can't get under ball. Point body and swing line 15 to 20 degrees left of target, and open clubface to point 15 to 30 degrees to right of target line. Loses some distance as flight higher than standard chip. Best addressed slightly towards toe of club. Fig 6.4.2.2 shows the address from in front: the feet are shown a little too far apart.

Some pros. More loft gives a softer landing. Natural. Little risk of double-hit. Sole becomes less catchy.

Some cons. From poorer lies, fluffs, thins and shanks possible; requires precise hit; divots on your lawn.

4.2.3 Almost square "Toed" chip – shaft more vertical, ball close to toes; club almost square, but aimed very slightly left of target

Not compulsory, but very useful, as it minimises disastrous fluffs and thinned shots. The lie should preferably be reasonably good, without much grass behind the ball. The ball is very close to your toes, and is addressed nearer the toe, not the centre of the club. The toe brushes the ground, but the rest of the sole is off the ground, and so the resistance during the brush with the grass is much less, since the amount of metal in contact with the turf is much smaller and less "catchy" than the conventional flat sole chip. The greater the loft of the club, the more it must be slightly turned in to the left, to counter the effect of the more vertical shaft, which is to fly the ball a little to the right, if aimed normally with the leading edge. Use the "toed" chip with any iron from 4 to wedges. Figs 6.4.2.3 – (1) and (2) show the address from behind and in front.

Some pros. Minimises risk and consequences of bad fluff or thin. Shank impossible. Reliable roll. Less precise strike needed. Good for shorter chips. No divots on lawn.

Some cons. Small directional adjustment needed (not hard). Slight double-hit risk. Sand-wedge toe slightly catchy. Unnatural.

4.2.4 Cut or open "toed" chip

Not at all essential. The highest flying and softest landing of all chips. For wedges only, similar to 4.2.3 above, but opened up. Use only where you are close to hole, and need a very soft landing over a bunker, say.

Some pros. Minimal risk of fluff, thin, shank or double-hit. Softest landing. No real divot.

Some cons. Distance not easy to control. Direction harder to estimate. Unnatural.

4.3 Other stroke choices close to green

4.3.1 Putt-chip

Highly recommended, particularly for longer handicaps. A different kind of chip, but with a putting action. The main difference from the "toed" chip of No 3 above is that your legs stay in the same position throughout, as in the standard putt. Usable with any iron, for shorter distances. Toe only on ground, and ball addressed and played from toe of club. Club must also be toed-in slightly to correct direction error, especially the greater the loft. Fig 6.4.3 – (1) shows the address.

Some pros. Little chance of fluff, thin or shank. Softish. OK on lawn. Not much to go wrong.

Some cons. Unnatural. Needs direction adjustment (not hard).

4.3.2 Putt

If the roll on the apron or closely cut fairway is reliable, and if the greens are fast and/or sloping, and it's windy, as often happens by the sea, a putt may be the best percentage option. Chapter 5 "Putting" details three possible putting actions – standard if near the hole, chip-putt from further away, or topspin putt from anywhere off the green. I find that the top-spin putt works very well provided one has the confidence to strike it positively, which can best be acquired from practice.

78

4.3.3 "Wood" or "Utility"

I'm sure these bigger-headed clubs have a role round the green, particularly from light rough when the grass grain is not against you; many golfers find them useful. I don't normally use them, and so won't tell you how to do it.

4.3.4 Soft flop pitch

Phil Mickelson's trade mark shot. Not a chip at all, but useful when you need absolute maximum height and soft landing. Use maximum loft wedge, laid heavily open. Usually played with full swing, which may be slow for shorter distances. If you can become good at this shot, it can give you a psychological advantage.

4.3.5 "Bellied" or "skulled" wedge

Handy when ball is up against a collar of longer grass, or for putting, if you have broken your putter, or your putting has deserted you!

5 Weighing up best shot choice

With so many different ways of playing a short shot, one can get thoroughly confused over which to choose. The second problem is knowing how hard to hit it. Both must be thought of at the same time, quickly and efficiently. Some specific elements are:

5.1 Your first landing point

may be typically a yard or so onto the green, or some other point on or short of the green. It should be a point that will produce a reliable run-on, and where small errors will not be magnified, but preferably diminished – e.g. playing for a small depression is much better than a hump, as the dip corrects small errors and vice-versa. Try to get the ball rolling before it encounters difficult slopes.

5.2 Speed and break

The usual considerations of speed and break apply, as for putting – speed of grass, height differences, wind, grain, etc, with the added complication of the first bounce.

5.3 Slope at the target first bounce

The slope at the target first bounce can be a vital factor. If it is appreciable, its effect on run-out distance will be much increased, because the incoming angle of the ball will be similar to the angle of the first bounce – it may run back, or even bounce back towards you in extreme cases.

5.4 Club loft and the ball flight

Dave Pelz has found that the lower the club's loft and the ball flight, the closer it will finish. This effect is further improved from a good lie, which involves less back-spin and less turf resistance than a tighter lie.

6 Judging the right strength
6.1 An instinctive way

Judging strength and then playing it with commitment and confidence are each difficult and vital. In the old days it was done by eye and feel, and it still is and can be today at all levels. If you had to roll or pitch a ball low or high just with your hand, you would know instinctively how much it needed for a particular flight and run-on, just as you should know instinctively how hard to toss a ball into a basket, or throw a dart at a dartboard. Try a simulated right underarm practice "toss". Then repeat this with one or two practice swings. Then, with as little delay as possible, play the shot. Try to keep the same tempo and rhythm on all chips (as with nearly all golf shots and see 6.3). For tight lies you will need more firmness of grip and stroke, and more positive acceleration through the ball.

6.2   A calibrated method

There is a way to remove some of the guesstimation as to swing length and carry. Go to flat ground, and set up markers every 2 yards say, and chip at standard rhythm and various calibrated swing lengths with different clubs, from say your 4-iron up to your most lofted wedge, using standard swing lengths, and you will see that the distance it carries is remarkably consistent in each case: note it down. You won't need to measure anything like all the many possible permutations, as you will see a clear pattern emerging. I will not give you any of my figures, since it may confuse or mislead, and in any case they would not apply exactly to you. By "standard swing lengths", I mean e.g. that you could use four swing lengths, namely, taking a reference point level with the outside of your right thigh and in line with: (1) the back of your right hand; (2) the junction of your hands; and (3) the middle of your left wrist and (4) your left elbow. Be aware of lining these points up with your dominant eye. These four positions or swing lengths equate to roughly equal increases in angle of left arm rotation to about 10, 20, 30 and 40 degrees, not unlike Dave Pelz's

81

method of distance control for part-strength wedges (Chapter 7 "Pitching") You can estimate or pace off the exact distance to your target landing point, and give the shot the correct swing length for the club and your own tempo. One or two practice swings, and then play the shot with confidence.

6.3 Rhythm and Tempo

These two ways of judging the strength will work if your rhythm and tempo are consistent. Rhythm should be even-paced, preferably a slight pause at the top of the backswing, and a positive stroke through the ball and beyond. Tempo means the speed of the swing – the chipping swing should take the same time for all swing lengths, on a count of say "one – two", or "one – pause – two". This will produce the slowest clubhead speeds for the shortest swings, and vice-versa, as in putting. Having decided how long your swing will be, trust your judgement, and do just that. For a good rhythm count "back – pause – through – down – up" so that you do not look up too early.

Chapter 7

Pitching

1   What is a pitch?

I define a pitch as a shot with wrist action – i.e. usually mainly cocking and uncocking, with a lofted club, usually a wedge, and a relatively high ball flight, and preferably a full finish. My pitch is very different from my chip, which has no hand or wrist action, and an abbreviated follow-through. The most lofted chip using an open, cut action can however fly higher and land softer than some standard smaller pitches.

   Pitches can fly as short as a few yards in the case of the special flop shot with a laid-open extra-lofted wedge, using a slow full swing, as perfected by Phil Mickelson (but this is not a standard pitch) up to a full pitch shot with a pitching wedge, and anything in between – i.e. a flight of a few yards up to however far you hit your wedge, using either a full shot, or a part-strength shot.

2   How hard to hit a part-strength pitching wedge.

Top players have always been very accurate with wedges as long as they had full shots to play. But in the mid-1970s Dave Pelz found that they were remarkably inaccurate on distance when faced with a part-strength pitch. His detailed findings and remedies are in his book *Dave Pelz's Short Game Bible* 1999, which covers virtually all aspects of the short game, except putting, in some 400 pages. I find it an outstandingly good and useful book, being based on some of the best golf research ever done.

Up to the 1970s US Tour pros were very accurate in direction control, but surprisingly erratic for distance at part-strength pitching. The pros recognized this weakness and, because of it, they often "laid the ball back" or up, to leave themselves a full wedge in. Pelz found a remedy which works very well for accuracy of carry distance. The only problem remaining now is the effect of spin, which is not easy for the pros to predict. But for them, there is usually less spin on a part-strength wedge than a full wedge, so it is now better for them, rather than worse, to be anything from around 30 to 90 yards away than say 120 yards. We ordinary golfers don't normally have the problem with heavy spin, and we can benefit greatly from improved distance control from the shorter ranges.

3   The solution

Pelz's solution was to carry at least two wedges, typically a standard pitching wedge, about 46 degrees for amateurs, and a sand wedge, about 56 deg. Pros might carry a gap wedge and a lob wedge in addition. Each wedge can be hit at say three or more part-strengths, and also in two different ways – either the standard square shot, or the open, cut wedge, which flies higher and lands softer, and carries about a quarter less far. With 3 or 4 wedges you can cover almost any carry distance, and you can cover most distances with only your two basic wedges. The strength, and so the distance of the shot's flight is determined by the length of the backswing.

For the *length of swing* Pelz uses a clock system, namely 7.30, which is 45 degrees up from the vertical; 9.00 (horizontal) and 10.30 (45 deg above horiz). These angles are taken to the angle which the left arm makes from the vertical at the address position. Two problems: (1) The left arms of pros will probably be straight in a part-strength "finesse" shot, and so there is no doubt as to whether you are measuring to the upper arm or forearm, and (2) For the pros a 10.30 swing is less than full, but for older or normal golfers, we may not be able to get as far as that, and if we do, our left arm may be bent, and do you measure to the forearm or the upper arm? A good compromise is to take the angle as the line joining the left shoulder centre and left hand centre. For the older or stiffer golfer I suggest using 7.00, 8.00, 9.00 and maybe 10.00 o'clock as the part-strength angles, if you can comfortably get that far with a part-strength swing. Figs 7.3 – (1, 2, 3 and 4) show these four "clock" positions, which are the same as going back by 30, 60, 90 and 120 degrees. The 10.00 o'clock position shown in the fourth shot is actually shown at 10.30.

Rhythm and Tempo. All "finesse" part-strength wedges should be stroked with a similar easy rhythm and tempo. All the different backswing lengths should take about the same length of time from start to impact, so that clubhead speed at impact should range from slowest for the 7.00 o'clock swing to fastest for the 10.00 o'clock backswing. I recommend the briefest pause at the top of the backswing to prevent snatching, and to get a good feeling that you have swung back the right distance.

A valuable feature of these shots is that the finish is identical in all cases. The exact finish position may either be with the wedge pointing vertically upwards, as in Fig 7.3 – (5), or continuing on as in Fig 7.3 (6), as Pelz recommends. The golfer has gradually come up, from the moment when the club is horizontal roughly halfway through the follow-through. He is pointing down the line, with weight on the front foot, and back foot fully turned, and pointing into the ground, as in each of Figs 7.3 – (5) and (6). It is called a finesse swing, because there is less coil and uncoil, and so less power, and more accuracy and consistency. Distance control is got purely from the length of the backswing. To work well, the tempo and rhythm of all lengths of swing must remain the same.

To find out your own distances, go to a flat area, preferably on a calm day of average temperature, and hit many shots at the various swing lengths and types, and measure off the carry distances. A good way is to place tennis balls at fixed distances at 5 or 10 yard intervals, and estimate and note the yardages carried, which should be consistent for all shots as mentioed above, struck true. As with chipping and most other shots, it is useful to have a slight pause at the top of the backswing.

4   Special Short Game Shots

In his *Short Game Bible* Pelz tells you just about all you need to know about the short game – not just the standard shots, but he covers many kinds of special and difficult situations.

5 Ball position

Pelz stresses that it is easy to be misled by relating ball position to the toes, because a heavily turned-out left (front) foot for example can make the ball look further back than it really is. The better way to gauge it is from the centres of the ankles. Pelz stresses the importance of ball position, and explains what can go wrong.

6 Greenside Bunkers

These shots are very like pitches, so should be considered here. Some variations:

6.1 Standard bunker escape

Pelz has done much research, and disproved the old dogma that you have to hit the sand 2 or 3 inches behind the ball. He recommends an open set-up, with every part of the body and the swing line pointing 15 to 20 degrees left of target. The clubface should aim 25 to 30 degrees right of target. The ball just inside the left heel, looked at from in front square-on. The club should enter the sand some 4" to 5" behind the ball, and take a shallow divot of sand 10" or so long. This method allows more margin for error than trying to hit closer to the ball, and so produces more consistent results.

You can then calibrate your carry distances with your sand-wedge (and other lofted clubs) for different backswing lengths, as with your part-strength pitches. A pro would carry a sand-wedge about 16 yards with a 9.00 o'clock or 90 degree swing. We would probably carry it less far.

6.2 Longer greenside bunker shot

If we find ourselves outside the maximum range for a sand-wedge, we should go for a less-lofted club, which will carry it further with the same swing. There is no need to worry about loss of "bounce" in the sand because your normal wedge or other lofted iron has no bounce, but in opening it up by 28 degrees or so, you get ample "bounce". If you haven't tried this shot before with say an 8-iron, you may worry at first. But with practice you will realize it does work. It is the best way to play a longer greenside bunker shot.

6.3 Ball buried or partly buried

All books tell you what to do, and usually agree that you should generally take your normal wedge, to allow it to cut much more steeply into the sand. I find that to exaggerate this action works well. If you play the ball a long way back, even well outside your right foot, and come very steeply down on it, not far off vertically, you can use your sand-wedge, or wedge, and even if it is fully buried, it should come out well, with some height, and with some control of distance. Try it in a practice bunker, until you master it!

6.4 Lipless bunkers

Not often found, but if forward escape is almost impossible, and there is no lip at back or side, a good way is to putt! (Not exactly right for a Pitching chapter, but we're talking about bunkers.) Pelz says the chip-putt should be used. But I say that an even better result comes from trying a heavy topspin putt, which I find more reliable.

Chapter 8

Long game and common elements for most golf shots

This chapter deals with the "long game" and also some **common elements** running through all golf shots in section 8. The Long Game could be defined as full shots, which can fall under two headings:

1 Power shots

They use full coil and uncoil, and full weight transfer. Used most commonly for the driver off the tee when good distance is a factor. But the greatest mistake is to think you have to thrash it! For a normal full power shot you would still be advised to keep your tempo well below the swing speed which you **could** generate. If you are timing the ball really well on the day, you could risk going a little faster, for a little more distance, as long as the swing is not too fast up to almost impact, with the extra speed **seeming** to come in **after** the ball has been struck.

2 Full "Finesse" shots

A very similar swing – almost a power shot, but a little less coil and less than maximum weight transfer. Why use it? Because it should be more consistent as to both length and directional accuracy. A full finesse swing can be used for any club, and is likely to carry roughly 10% shorter than your full power swing.

Another way to take something off a full shot can be to use a slightly reduced-length backswing, as in the part-strength wedge pitching distance-control system in Chapter 7 "Pitching". The important thing with these, as with virtually all golf shots, is to be positive on the follow-through, and to complete it.

3   Possible elements in full power swings

A large number of movements can contribute power. Here is my comprehensive list. They do not all have to be used – indeed there are some which are better avoided. Ben Hogan in his classic *The Modern Fundamentals of Golf* thought of the swing as a chain reaction starting at the feet, and where they contact the ground. The great teacher David Leadbetter in *The Golf Swing* thinks on similar lines. Starting at the feet, and working upwards eventually to the hands, possible elements are:

3.1   Feet/ground reaction

A vital ingredient: we need to feel that we are pushing the planet to our right as our weight transfers to the left at the start of the downswing. This feeds a lot of power into our legs. If we were on ice, with slippery shoes on, we couldn't push the world, and would lose a vital power source.

3.2 Large muscles of the legs

If we are really using these muscles, we will feel them working, especially the thigh muscles. Good strong legs are indispensible for good golf, both for the swing, and for getting round.

3.3 Body rotation

For a full power swing, the average golfer's hips should go round by about 30+ to 45 degrees, but his shoulders roughly 90 degrees, producing upper body coil, in the backswing, and the shoulders should finish pointing at least straight down the line. Young flexible golfers will do this easily, while older stiffer golfers may struggle.

3.4 Weight transfer

It is impossible to achieve maximum power unless you include good weight transfer in your swing. This means getting much of your weight onto the back foot at the initial "top of the backswing". Then the key move is to initiate the transfer at the top of the backswing, by getting into a "pulling" position, which involves a forward movement of the hips and knees. By the time the club reaches the ball, much of the weight has moved onto the left (front) foot, until at the finish there should be very little weight on the right (back) foot. This contrasts sharply with the "reverse pivot" from which many golfers suffer, and causes much loss of power and other problems – too much weight stays on the front foot towards the top of the backswing, and then transfers to the back foot at the finish, and they "fall off it" i.e. backwards and to their right. Figs 8.3.4 –(1) and (2) show the two positions at the top of the backswing before and after the weight shift forward into the pulling position. Figs 8.3.4 – (3) and (4) show the same for the 74-year-old author, who cannot get as far back any more!

3.5   Arm movement

In addition to body rotation, the arms have to be moved an extra amount relative to the chest, round, but essentially upwards, to promote a wide arc to the backswing. We need to look first at the role of each arm separately, before considering them together. The **left arm** has two conflicting tasks: on one hand it has (1) to give width to the arc of the swing, which is vital, and (2) it arguably provides stability to the exact position of the clubhead, so that it should come back to precisely where it started at the address, and a good contact can be made in the middle of the clubface. To achieve both these ends, many think it best to keep the left arm dead straight. But on the other hand, a straight left arm provides little power in itself: more power can be got from the left arm if the left elbow is bent to a degree. Whether the advantages of the straight left arm outweigh the advantages of the to-a-degree-bent left arm is debatable – see Chapter 3 "17 Common Conceptions questioned" – CC 3. In David Leadbetter's book *Lessons from the Golf Greats* he features 25 of the world's top golfers, and 24 of them have some degree of bend at their left elbow. The only exception is Ernie Els, who has a superb swing, and is strong and long, and doubtless does not need the extra strength from a bent left elbow.

The right arm provides most of the arm power whatever you do with your left arm. The position of the right elbow at the initial top of the backswing is hotly debated. Many commentators don't like the "flying right elbow". But Jack Nicklaus uses it, so it must be alright in itself. It tends to widen the swing arc, which will help, especially with the driver. If you assume the hands to reach a given position at the top of the backswing, it follows that the right elbow can be in any position from very flying to very close in. What is far more important is that at the start of the downswing the right elbow is pulled in close to the body, so that it gets into a "pulling" position. You need to feel you are "pulling" the club from the top, rather than "pushing" it. Pulling something is often easier and more powerful than pushing it. Much power is contributed by good right arm action. The further back your swing can comfortably go, the more speed and power can be delivered, other things equal.

3.6 Wrist and hand actions

There are three possible movements:

3.6.1 Wrist cocking, uncocking and recocking

This movement is very desirable in every shot, except chips and putts, and is virtually indispensible. Most golfers can cock their wrists through about 90 degrees. The "Square to Square" theory took off principally in the 1970s, encouraging golfers to keep the left hand square to their left arm: keep your wristwatch pointing straight forward at the top of the backswing, and then in the follow-through to do the same with an imaginary wristwatch on your right arm. This should largely eliminate the other two possible movements – hingeing and forearm rotation. Fig 8.3.6.1 shows wrist cocking on its own, without any other movement.

3.6.2 Wrist hingeing

If you put your hands in front of you with hands and fingers flat together in a modified prayer position with your fingers pointing away from you, and then move both hands to right and left, you are hingeing. This can give some extra power. It is possible to swing with a lot of hinge – the wrists can hinge by up to 90 degrees each way. But most people find it unnatural. Its great advantage is that it can keep the clubface very much more square to the target throughout the swing, which improves directional accuracy. Against that, it does not feel natural to many, and small errors of timing cause the loft angle at impact to vary, which will hamper distance control. Wrist hingeing was warmly endorsed by Mindy Blake in his two thought-provoking books *The Golf Swing of the Future* 1972 and *Golf: The Technique Barrier* 1978. He asserted that the great J H Taylor used this action. Mindy Blake used it very effectively himself. But you can manage very well with little or no wrist hinge in any golf shot. Figs 8.3.6.2 – (1) and (2) show the wrists hingeing to the author's maximum back and forward, without any other movement.

3.6.3 Forearm rotation

This is a potential power source of some force. But timing has to be very accurate, and is not easy. For most it is more trouble than it is worth.

It is hard enough timing the cocking movements, and a lot harder if this rotation is added. The best way to time wrist movement is not to try to do so by brain control. Much the better way is to leave it to nature, which is much more likely to return the club with its face angle the same as it was at address – small differences lead to large errors: if one is tense, the wrist cock tends to un-cock too late, resulting in an open face, and a slice, push, or even shank. The one time when forearm rotation is recommended is for the deliberate hook, when the "rolling over" of the forearms and hands, with an "in to out" swing and a closed stance should produce a sharp hook. Figs 8.3.6.3 – (1) and (2) show the author's forearms rotating to their maximum without any other movement, except in the second picture the arms have unintentionally moved forward a little too much.

There is another possible hand movement, which is not necessarily bad. Many golfers, good and less good, let go of the club at the top of the backswing. The pads of both hands may come away from the club grip, allowing the shaft to go back an extra 20 degrees or so compared with how far it would go back if the grip were tightly held. Then somewhere in the downswing they resume their normal grip, as Sergio Garcia is said to do. This gives some extra whip, speed and power. For all full shots use a lightish grip, unless you have to go through heavy or wiry turf immediately after contact.

4 "Shaping" the shot

Many top players like to hit their favourite draw or

fade much of the time. We lesser mortals hit our slices and hooks, when we are trying to hit it straight. We may have a tendency to fade or draw, or worse. The ideal is to hit a straight flying ball as standard, and to be able to bend it as needed! For the deliberate fade or draw the degree of bend needs to be controllable. The chances are you are bending it away from trouble. There are various recommended ways to produce a fade or draw. I believe the simplest and most reliable is for a draw to line the club up with the final target, typically say the centre of the fairway, and to point the whole system very slightly right – i.e with a very slightly closed stance, and swing the club normally along the line your system is pointing at, to produce a slight draw. The reverse for a fade. These shots should be practised to build confidence.

5   Driver

Maximum distance comes from using all these elements, except those that are not recommended. Normally use a full swing with full coil and uncoil, and a lightish grip. There may be three cases with the driver:

5.1   Maximum distance

Use all the recommended elements. Keep the grip light – a tight grip gives less wrist action. Do not try to thrash it! Be extra slow and wide on your backswing. If you are timing it well on the day, you could swing a fraction faster, but preferably mostly around and after impact. At all parts of the backswing and the first half of the downswing keep your speed down to about 50% of the speed you could generate. From there gradually increase speed to 60% before impact, trying to reach 70% beyond impact. (Actually the club will be slowed by impact, but you need to feel that your maximum effort and speed comes after impact.) Go on to a full finish, remembering that the follow-through is the most important part of the swing! Use this maximum swing only when you really need to.

5.2   Normal full swing

Very much like No. 1 above, except it should be an easy rhythmic affair, with little apparent effort, but a full swing. It won't matter if you are 5 to 10% shorter – you will be accurate, and still have gone a good distance. Use this swing when the extra few yards don't matter.

5.3   Part-strength driver

Modern drivers are so easy to hit, being so forgiving. You may feel more confident with your driver, or it may be just too far for your next-down wood. Or it may be a hole where it is essential to finish on the fairway at all costs. In the old days the driver was the riskier, wilder club than the old "spoon" or modern 3-wood, the latter being recommended if you needed a straighter but shorter shot. But today you can choke down on your driver, by e.g. taking a less-than-full swing, and/or choking down on the grip. But you must give it a positive hit, with a proper finish.

6   Full shots from sand

If lie is good, first strike must be on ball, not sand, to get the distance with club selected. If struck right, ball first and then sand, backspin will be more than usual, so expect fair screw-back after landing say on up-sloping green (they usually are). If the ball is sitting up nicely on the sand it can be more of a sweeping action, but if it is not quite so good, it should be more of a downward strike, and your wood or utility may not be suitable.

7 The dreaded shank or socket

Apart from "the yips", can you think of a worse golfing ailment? Console yourself because they say you have to be quite a good golfer to shank! A true story to confirm this is in Bernhard Langer's *My Autobiography* 2002. He turned pro at only fifteen, and immediately went out onto the practice ground. The first 50 balls he hit were **all** shanks! That didn't stop him from becoming one of the greatest ball-strikers. He must have found the remedy there and then.

As you know, golfers hardly dare breathe the word. If you are not afflicted, you don't even want to know about the disease. To my generation it was the "J. Arthur", short for the film impresario, and sometimes shortened to just "J". I've done it all too often, and I know that it costs you more than 1 shot on average each time. I can't give you the complete answer, because there are more ways than one to shank. I believe that a prime cause is being afraid to execute the hand action properly: one is tense, and so the uncocking of the wrists towards impact is frozen, and the ball does not "see enough of" the flat, square face of the iron, but too much of the socket. In this case, an almost-shank would be a se-vere push, as the club is much too open at impact.

The way to avoid this particular common shanker's fault is (1) to make sure your wrists are suitably loose, and operate correctly, completing their action, and (2) **want** to hit the ball, rather than being afraid of it!

Unfortunately shanking can happen with irons in almost any shot – full shots, pitches, bunker shots and even chips – I know, because I've done it. One relief is that it is virtually impossible with most woods, utilities and putters! Pelz has a remedy – standing further away, and a gadget to cure the problem.

8   Common Elements for (almost) all golf shots

These may fall under two headings:

8.1   Before you play

In roughly the order you should do them, these things could be described as part of your "Pre-Shot Routine":

8.1.1   Weigh up your next shot

Weigh up your next shot and decide exactly what you will do. Covered in detail in 1 and 2 of Chapter 4 "Managing your game".

8.1.2   Go through the rest of your Pre-Shot Routine

This and the "Pre-Shot Ritual" which follows are well described in *Dave Pelz's Short Game Bible*, section 12.7, which has advice additional to mine, including the importance of imagining and visualizing your shot. Then, with at least one practice swing, get the feel of the perfect swing and distance, particularly if it is a part-

99

strength shot, and its *rhythm and tempo.* As to rhythm, I like to pause at the top to avoid snatching, and to feel good during the actual swing that I have the right length of swing for a less-than-full shot. Tempo should be your natural pace – we all have one – and I recommend that all shots are played considerably slower than the speed you could generate (see below).

A word of caution: there are many things you should think about before any shot. You have to strike a balance between covering at least all the important things, while not being a slow player.

Train yourself to think quickly, but efficiently. When you are (quickly) ready to play the shot, get on with it: it will not only speed up your play, but produce a better result.

8.1.3 Take up your stance and address

First line up your club along your target line if it is a square shot. Many errors of direction are due to poor lining up, especially among ladies! I think the reason is that ladies sometimes rush, to keep out of the way of the men! It is best done by laying the sole on the ground (unless it is a "toed" chip) while holding it loosely with one or both hands. When you think it is pointing in the right direction, put your grip on. I haven't said anything about grip variations. I believe the hands should whenever possible be in a natural or "neutral" position. If you lean forward slightly and let your arms hang loosely in front of you, you will probably find that the backs of your hands are facing slightly forwards, showing about two knuckles each, viewed from in front of you. This should be your normal grip. For grip strengths, Chapter 3 – CC 8 and elsewhere gives my ideas on grip strengths. Then set your feet and body, remembering that the reference point for ball position fore and aft should be to the middle of your ankles, not your toes, which tends to make the ball go a little farther back to the true centre – better for wedges taking divots according to Pelz. Try to take a deep breath, and expel some of it just before you play, particularly on long shots.

8.1.4 Pre-Shot Rituals

Pelz says that this is not about hitting the ball, but training your subconscious to perform the proper rhythm when you're scared. You will benefit from a consistent never-changing ritual, which you should ingrain in your practice sessions: 8.1.2 shows where to find details.

8.2   During the stroke

The brain can't think of much more than one thing at a time, with a maximum of 3 things. On the golf course you shouldn't think of more than one, or two at the most. The thinking should be done during practice sessions. Good things to think of while playing a shot are rhythm or tempo and/or keeping hub height steady, and/or positive follow-through.

8.2.1 Rhythm and Tempo

For most golf shots I recommend an easy rhythm and tempo, preferably with a pause at the end of the backswing, to avoid sudden snatching. For long shots on the way down start at 50% of the speed you could generate, rising to 60%, and then 70% at first impact, and trying for maximum speed of 80% a little beyond the ball.

8.2.2 Keep hub height and position steady

Vital for all shots, though less relevant on putts, so as to avoid thin and heavy shots, and to hit ball in centre of clubface. It helps to think consciously of it.

8.2.3 What to do with your eyes?

Chapter 3 CC 7, and Chapter 5 – "Putting" section 3.3 tell you what to do with your eyes in most circumstances. Sensible use of the eyes should contribute greatly to avoiding pulling your body out of position through your eyes following the ball too soon or in a wrong way.

8.2.4 A positive and full follow-through

I believe this is one of the greatest contributors to good golf. It is fully described and justified in Chapter 3 paras CC 4 and 5, and in the Appendix. Every part of the preparation and swing is important, but I believe the follow-through is particularly so. I believe that one can get away with less than perfect things happening before impact, whose effect can be lessened with a good full follow-through. Try to feel that you are driving through right to the finish.

Part 2

Non-technical

Chapter 9

World Golf from 1890s to 2010 and beyond

This chapter is my view of aspects of the game's development since the 1890s, and suggests where it may go in the years ahead. I am not going to look at whether the Dutch with their "Kolv" in the 13th century or the Scots were the first to play the game. I suspect that Kolv was a rather different game, played mainly on frozen waterways, where normal flight, carry and run-out were less involved. Since the Scots were playing golf as early as the 15th century, I would think we can credit them with the first playing of the game more as we know it.

With the notable exception of the Royal Blackheath club, founded in 1608, which predates the Royal and Ancient in 1754, I believe golf was largely a Scottish game until the last decade or two of the 19th century, when an era of building courses south of the border started. This spread of the game helped bring about for the first time a non-Scottish impact at the top, in the shape of J H Taylor from the south-west of England, and Harry Vardon from Jersey. They, and the third of the "Great Triumvirate" – the Scot, James Braid, were all born within 14 months of each other from 1870 – see Fig 9.

Up to the mid 1890s, and well beyond it, the golf professional was regarded rather as a working man with a great skill. They were usually attached to a club, and to a fair degree undertook the normal duties of a club pro, selling, repairing and possibly making clubs. They were quite unlike the modern tournament touring professional. There were "big money matches", and had been for many years, featuring pros, and sometimes amateurs. The Amateur was a very different beast, being a gentleman who could afford to play golf for pleasure and love of the game.

By the mid-1890s golf started to attract more interest, having pushed south of the border, heightened by the rivalry between J H Taylor and Harry Vardon, and then James Braid. A significant development in technique occurred in 1895. J H had won the Open in 1894 and 1895, and in 1896 he tied with Vardon for a play-off. The two had markedly different swings, both different again from the "Old St Andrews swing" prevalent until that time. The old swing was not vastly different from the swing of today, except that as well as turning your back on the aimline in the backswing, you turned your hips a similar amount. This did not give the powerful upper body coil now used by all top golfers. Taylor's different new style was to be very open, with his feet pointing well to the left, at the same time swinging through the ball along the line, with coil. Vardon was arguably the forerunner of the conventional modern movement. Vardon beat Taylor in the 1896 play-off, and won again in '98 and '99, and became the greatest of the Great Triumvirate. And so it was Vardon's action which became the model which virtually all golfers followed. Had Taylor won, things might have been different. Golfers might find Taylor's action less gainly, and harder to replicate.

The other major influence was the starting of the game in the USA. The first course was built in about 1880. Americans realized they did not have the knowledge and experience for course design and teaching, so they imported professionals largely from Scotland with little difficulty, which got the game going quickly. But the biggest accelerator was a US tour by the famed Harry Vardon in 1900, lasting several months, and creating huge new interest. Coincidentally it was the 7-year-old Francis Ouimet who was captivated by Vardon, the world's greatest golfer.

Vardon then in the early 1900s had serious health problems, which prevented him from winning the major championships even more often. But he recovered, and in 1913 made his second tour of the USA, culminating in the US Open, for which the hot favourites were the Englishmen Vardon and the powerful Ted Ray. After six rounds, including two qualifying rounds, there was a triple tie involving Vardon, Ray, and the young unkown American amateur Francis Ouimet, all having seen off the strong field of all the best expatriate Scottish-Americans and home-grown Americans, both professional and amateur. When Ouimet managed narrowly to beat the two Englishmen in the 36 hole play-off, it was the most significant moment ever for American golf. Ouimet was the first home-grown American to win a "major" Championship. It lead to a huge explosion in interest, and the feeling that the new land could now challenge the old masters.

The first great golfer to profit was Walter Hagen (b. 1892). Hagen was followed by the immortal Bobby Jones, and also Gene Sarazen, both b. 1902. And the rest is history. Home-grown Americans, largely those three, won the oldest trophy – the Open – with only one break, from 1921 to 1933. It was mostly that Open record which made people think that in the post-Vardon, post-Triumvirate era, they were now the new masters. This impression was reinforced by American successes in their own US Open and US PGA Championships, the latter effectively closed to non-Americans. When Bobby Jones created the Masters in 1934 it was the moment when the fourth "Major" had arrived, and this is the same to this day.

There is no doubt that American golf was at the top for most of the 70 years from the First World War until about the early 1980s. This view was encouraged by the fact that Americans dominated the four Majors to a large degree. However, one should perhaps ask whether this dominance was as overwhelming as is commonly thought. Three of the four Majors are played in America: up until about the mid-1980s, the entry for the three US Majors was very largely American pros. This made it much more likely that Americans would win, and take most of the top places. It was only since then that they have gradually opened the fields up to include most or all the world's top golfers that the Americans have lost that important advantage. But even today I reckon they still have a significant advantage. The world's top 100 or so golfers, who make up the core of the fields, are chosen from the world rankings, which are based on money earnings. These are highest in America, and so I believe they flatter American pros, and those who play there. Conversely one might argue that because there are so many good Americans – strength in depth – it is harder to stand out over there, since more people are after the much larger spoils.

One could argue that the most meaningful Major over most of the 90 or 120 years in question has been the oldest, the Open, because in many of those years it was the only Major to have a more truly representative field of most of the world's best golfers. But from Sam Snead's win in 1946 to Arnold Palmer's first win in 1961 Americans of quality were very thinly represented, except for Ben Hogan's win in 1953. We can thank Palmer for gradually turning the Open once again into the most important and representative Major in the calendar from the early 1960s to the late 20th century. The roll-call of winners and top performers was not as strongly American as one would think in many years since 1933. Americans enjoyed being top dogs, and did not like it when for example Bobby Locke went over there and proved to be at least as good as most of them.

From the Second World War the Ryder Cup was mostly won by the Americans. I believe this was because British golf was more depleted by the war than American golf, and also that Great Britain and Ireland went into the Cup believing they were likely to lose, thinking they had less strength, which is debatable, and less depth, undoubtedly true. Accordingly in the mid-70s it was thought that if it was to survive it was necessary to strengthen the GB and

Ireland side by bringing in the Europeans. This did not quite work immediately, but a turning point came, arguably in 1983 in America, but more obviously in 1985 at The Belfry, probably inspired quite largely by Tony Jacklin's two Major wins thirteen years earlier, and his becoming Captain, and also by Seve and his five Major wins. Since then the tables have been conclusively turned, with Europe being the dominant Ryder Cup force. The somewhat golden days of the 80s and 90s when British and European golfers won the Open and the Masters quite often have not been repeated much since Tiger Woods got going. But the latest signs are that English and Irish golfers are coming up strong, but have yet to deliver the ultimate prizes more often.

Another notable yardstick is the President's Cup – USA vs The Rest of the World. In its short life USA have rather dominated, which is a little surprising, since the Internationals have mostly been highly ranked, and have done well in world golf. On paper the Internationals have possibly had a slight edge over the Europeans in these years. But the Europeans have punched above their apparent weight, while the Internationals have punched below theirs. Could it be that the Internationals are a less cohesive and team-spirited bunch than the older two groups? Maybe the World Rankings arguably inflate the Americans and the Internationals slightly, at the expense of Europeans who don't play as much in the USA? I believe Americans have a slight edge on standardised techniques and athletic fitness, while British Isles and southern European golfers rely a little more on their considerable natural flair.

My suggestion for throwing more light on this conundrum is to have a new event. On paper these three major groupings – USA, Europe and Internationals – should be fairly evenly matched. It might not be a good idea if there were some sort of three-cornered match-play event between these three teams played at the same time. But another way might be to set up a new strokeplay event between the three teams. Make it 72 holes with teams of twelve, played in 3-balls, one player from each team, the best 10 scores in each round to count. This has advantages – it allows for the odd injury; second it is easy to divide by 10, giving an understandable score, to one decimal point, e.g. 70.2, and also it means that every player would know that their score, however disappointing, might count. The results would give a better idea as to the relative strengths of the three main powers. Of course over many years there might spring up a new force in world golf, such as an Asian grouping of some kind. But this format would easily accommodate a fourth group.

Women's golf

Another thought of mine concerns women's golf. Top women players have made huge strides over the last 40 years or so in two main areas, I believe. Before about the 1970s I would guess that women pros and amateurs had more unconventional actions than today, there now being more conformity to accepted swing actions. The second thing that they have improved a lot is the short game from 100 yards in, including putting. I would suggest that top women pros are now close to the top men, and possibly better at accuracy and at certain ranges from the lofted clubs down to the short game. I wonder whether the day is approaching when top women may get closer to competing with top men. You might say this is impossible, because men are considerably stronger. They are, and this makes a vital difference. I would guess that women are at least 10% or so shorter in average carry and total distance, maybe more, but let us take 10%, as it is a convenient number.

This discrepancy makes a huge difference at many holes, such as longer par 4s and many par 5s. Take a 470 yard par 4: the average top man will hit the ball say 285 yards or more, leaving less than 200 yards, unless he is well off the fairway centre. His approach shot will need roughly a 5 or 6 iron. The average top woman will drive say 256 yards, leaving at least 214 yards, for which the most likely club will be a metal wood. It will be much harder to stop the ball quickly from the longer ranges, and to get the same accuracy. On the other hand, the women's driving will be more accurate. But men can stop the ball more readily.

With a wedge it is possible that the women may be more accurate: they can hit wedges a little less far, but they have noticeably less problem with backspin, making for better distance control. For many of the smaller shots around the green, and all the putting, there is no reason why women should not become at least as good as men. There are signs that this is already happening.

Overall I don't think that women will be able to compete effectively with men from the same tees. But there is no reason why it should not be a level playing field if women could use their own tees at about 10% shorter distance. The exact positioning of hazards and carries would need to be thought out carefully. There could be a trial event on the calendar. Alternatively or additionally, there could be a new Mixed Foursomes or Mixed Fourballs format. Fourballs would work better with the 10% tee placements, but separate tees need not be a problem for Mixed Foursomes.

The greatest of the All Time Great Men

Many followers of most sports like to speculate as to who were the best of all time. I am not going to start before the 1890s because the game was too small and hardly international – the early experts were virtually all Scottish. But by then the entry for the Open had become larger, and with more Englishmen playing. The American Open was first played in 1894, and it was largely expatriate Scots who won it for a time. The table Fig 9 shows the dates of birth from 1869 of 65 of the world's best men golfers who were successful from the 1890s. All the golfers in this list have won at least two Majors, but five of them have won only one Major – de Vicenzo, Woosnam, Couples, Love and Duval, who stand out because of their stature on the world scene in various ways – all but De Vicenzo and Love were No 1 in the World. Colin Montgomerie hasn't won a Major (yet), but he is outstandingly the best man never to have done so. He is surely a much better golfer than many on the list who have. His outstanding record in the Ryder Cup as the best European, and his eight wins, seven consecutive, in the European Order of Merit at a time when European golf was at the top or near the top is unlikely ever to be equalled. I have not included ten golfers who have won two Majors since the early days: they are nearly all Americans, and they won at times when those Majors did not mostly have significant international fields – several were the rather inaccessible-at-the-time US PGA Championship.

In weighing up who were the All Time Greats, or the Greatest of the All Time Greats, it might be useful to ask:

1. Who were the Men to Beat (MTBs)? and
2. Who were the men who Beat the Man to Beat (BMBs)?

I believe that the All Time Greats can be thought of as all falling broadly into one or other of these two categories.

The Men to Beat

JH Taylor was the first, but he was dominant only between 1894 and 1896. Harry Vardon then displaced JH by beating him in the 1896 Open play-off, and then consolidated his position. But Vardon fell seriously ill for a few years in the early 1900s, and this gave James Braid the chance to supplant Vardon, if only temporarily. Braid won his five Opens between 1901 and 1910, coming very close in the others, by when Vardon was back at the top again, despite a tremor in his right arm, which affected his putting.

The Great Triumvirate had monopolized the top of game for some twenty years, but in 1914, with all three in their early to mid-forties, and the Great War declared, it was the turn of Walter Hagen, then 21. Hagen was very much the Man to Beat until about 1925, when the 23-year old amateur Bobby Jones replaced Hagen with his seven great Open wins to add to his six Amateur titles. After Jones retired in 1930, having won the "Grand Slam" of Open and Amateur Championships there was a slight vacuum, filled largely by Gene Sarazen who won four of his seven majors between 1932 and 1935, and must have been The Man to Beat at that time.

For the next few years the spoils were shared, as there was no single dominant figure among Shute, Cotton, Horton Smith and Demaret, until in the early 1940s the great class of 1912 started to fire, first with Byron Nelson, The Man to Beat in the early 40s. Both Sam Snead, who won his seven Majors from age 30 to 42, and Ben Hogan with his nine Majors from 33 to 41 were late developers. My pick for The Man to Beat is Ben Hogan because of his serious car accident in 1949, and his immaculate long game precision. He was not renowned for his putting. Snead had one of the loveliest swings ever seen.

From the Snead/Hogan era up to 1954 there was a short lull, partly filled by the Locke/Thomson era, when from 1949 to 1958 they each won the Open four times. The Open between 1946 and the early 1960s has been somewhat devalued through low American participation, until Arnold Palmer's support from 1960 caused the Americans to take part in ever-increasing numbers. But I feel it was nevertheless arguably at least as significant then as the three US Majors, as the best players from around the world competed, which they did not do in the three US Majors, which were largely confined to Americans. The Americans certainly had most of the very top players from about 1915 to 1954, and then in the 60s and 70s.

A new breed burst onto the scene from the end of the 1950s in the shape of "The Big Three" – Palmer, Player and Nicklaus. At first, and for some five years until about 1964 Palmer was "The Man to Beat". But from then until the late 70s it was always Nicklaus as the MTB. An important word about Gary Player. He was, I believe, the outstanding "Man who Beat the Man to Beat" of all time. In view of the very stiff competition he faced from first Palmer and then Nicklaus and later Trevino, I don't think he should be regarded as a Man to Beat for a consistent and appreciable length of time. But his record is superb – nine Majors, and some 160 tournament wins all around the world, showing how well he handled all conditions. He is the supreme fighter and match-player, as his record in the World Matchplay confirms. Tony Jacklin was at the very top briefly.

Lee Trevino almost ranks as a MTB, but Nicklaus was probably still that man, although Trevino notched up his six Major wins in the Nicklaus era of dominance, and so he pushed him hard, and was a brilliant golfer. After Nicklaus came Tom Watson in the late 70s as the MTB, with his eight Majors, five of them in the Open, which at that time was the premier event. Watson's reign came to an end on losing the 1984 Open at St Andrew's to Seve, after which he had trouble for many years with holing the 5-footers which he had so often knocked in (and see below). Seve then became the MTB, with his five Majors and his dashing play, brilliant touch and recoveries.

The next man on the scene was Nick Faldo from

the late 80s to the early 90s, when he won both the Open and the Masters three times each, and was undoubtedly the MTB. Faldo, now Sir Nick, reached these heights by hard work, consistency and brilliance – the best British golfer since Harry Vardon, surpassing Sir Henry Cotton. One should perhaps consider Greg Norman. He won only two Majors, the Open, but was cruelly "robbed" three times as he was on the verge of winning three more, apart from a few others that slipped away. There was a time, between the Faldo dominance and the emergence of Tiger Woods during the mid 90s, when Norman was the world No. 1, and arguably the MTB.

But since his huge win in the 1997 Masters at 21, Tiger Woods has been the most outstanding of all MTBs having, at the time of writing, June 2010, recorded fourteen professional Major victories. He has doubtless had the greatest grip on world golf of any man, and it is anybody's guess how many more Majors he will accumulate. Currently the only man who can challenge Woods in golfing brilliance is Phil Mickelson, who at June 2010 is on four Majors, but turning 40, which is still young these days. No other "young up and coming" player appears in my list after Padraig Harrington who is nearly 39 already. None of the young lions have shown as yet. How long can Woods and the others keep them at bay?

Who are the Greatest Greats?

There are three who should pick themselves – Bobby Jones, Jack Nicklaus and Tiger Woods, and few would argue. Bobby Jones's career was hampered by poor health, and cut short by early retirement at 28. His seven pro Majors were from the only two Majors available to him, in addition to his six Amateur Majors. One need say no more about Nicklaus and Woods.

A key question is: should any others join these three, and if so, who? I believe that in age order, the closest candidates are:

Harry Vardon. Won seven Opens, when only one Major was fully available. Had a long period of illness in what should have been his most productive middle period. On returning his right arm tremor affected his putting, but he still won. The strength of competition was not as great then. I feel he should be up there with the obvious three.

Walter Hagen. Won eleven Majors, when only three available. A consummate winner, though not a stylist – does it matter? Five of his wins were in the USPGA, then matchplay, which he particularly loved, with his unbounded confidence. He was up against Jones and Sarazen, but the rest-of-the-world challenge was more modest at that time. To me, not quite as strong a challenger as Harry Vardon.

Ben Hogan. Nine Majors. A late developer, with first win at 33 in 1946. He perfected ball control with his long game, which more than made up for his average putting. His serious car accident in 1949 didn't stop him from several Major wins after that. Competition at his time was not the very toughest, especially from overseas. He cannot be excluded on ball-striking grounds, but just possibly on his overall record.

Arnold Palmer. Seven Majors + one Amateur. A commanding figure who did a lot for the game. His shortish but brilliant record may not be quite as strong as some of the other top contenders.

Gary Player. Nine Majors. Although perhaps not the Man to Beat, since he was up against Palmer and Nicklaus, and Trevino, he beat the MTBs very many times, and has possibly the best around the world record in a very competitive era. He should not be excluded at all easily.

Tom Watson. eight Majors – so far – after his almost certain and deserved ninth in the 2009 Open a few weeks before his 60th birthday. From 1984 he continued to play great golf, but those 5-footers wouldn't drop as before. He too is hard to exclude.

The relative importance of each of the 4 Majors at different times

This has varied considerably over the years. Today (2010) they are all roughly equal in attracting similar top entries from the world's best golfers, and the only difference is that the Masters has a slightly smaller field. But the relative stature of the four events varies a little, due to their respective histories, and the golf has its distinctive character in all four cases. The book *The Majors* – see Chapter 2 – brilliantly captures the different flavour of each event for the 1998 season, which is similar today, and will always make a good read.

Before about 1990 I believe the Americans had two important advantages in Major accumulation. First they effectively kept low the numbers of non-Americans competing in their three Majors. Second, they were on home ground. The first advantage appears to have gone, but not altogether, because the Sony World Rankings are based on money earnings, and the amounts earned are usually higher in the USA. Americans might argue that there are more good players over there, which is probably true, and the money is more spread around. But I believe that the world rankings flatter the Americans to some degree, and that this is reflected in the Ryder Cup results. If this is true, it would make for slightly more Americans gaining entry to the Majors than otherwise. Looking at the four Majors in date order of foundation:

The Open

The first Major from 1860. Between the wars the Americans started to come, and to win it in all but one year from 1921 to 1933. The Open has probably remained the premier Major for world golfers at all times, while Americans have had their three home Majors, which have until relatively recently been confined effectively to Americans for the most part. Americans would see the three US Majors as more important than the Open at the times when their players dominated world golf, and before they started coming across in large numbers from about 1970, from which time the Open had the strongest fields of all, at least until recently, and is the most sought-after, although Americans would be particularly happy to win the hard-fought US Open.

US Open

From 1894. It has an enormous field of many thousands, who have to pre-qualify and then qualify. Until the emergence of European golf in the 1980s with their many wins in the Ryder Cup, Masters and the Open, the US Open was an almost all-

American affair, and so not a good test of world golf until it was opened up more recently. Courses are made very tough so that par is not easily broken.

US PGA

From 1916, and a matchplay event until 1957. It was restricted to USPGA pros, or those on the PGA tour, and so used to have very few non-Americans, and as such it was the least significant of the four. But in recent years the PGA have changed their approach to bring it fully in line with the world scene.

US Masters

From 1934. Originally an invitation event with smallish fields, and the only Major which does not rotate courses. Probably the third most prestigious. The delightful Augusta course is a different test, and slightly favours the man who draws the ball. But why not have different tests? They do in tennis, with its different surfaces.

Fig 9 – Birth dates of 65 of the best men golfers since the 1890s

1869-1871 Harold Hilton (Am) 1/69; James Braid 2/70; **Harry Vardon 5/70**; JH Taylor 3/71
72,73
74-76
77,78 Ted Ray 1877; Willie Anderson 1878
1879-1881
82,83
84-86
87,88 Jim Barnes 1887
1889-1891
92,93 **Walter Hagen 12/92**

121

94-96 Tommy Armour 1896

97,98

1899-1901 Craig Wood 11/01

1902,03 Gene Sarazen 2/02; **Bobby Jones (Am) 3/02**

04-06 Densmore Shute 10/04

07,08 Henry Cotton 1/07; Horton Smith 5/08

1909-1911 Jimmy Demaret 1910

12,13 Byron Nelson 2/12; Sam Snead 5/12; **Ben Hogan 8/12**; Ralph Guldahl 11/12

14-16

17,18 Bobby Locke 11/17

1919-1921 Julius Boros 3/20; Carey Middlecoff 1/21

22,23 Roberto de Vicenzo 4/23

24-26

27,28

1929-1931 Peter Thomson 8/29; **Arnold Palmer 9/29**; Gene Littler 7/30; Billy Casper 6/31

32,33

34-36 **Gary Player 11/35**

37,38

1939-1941 Lee Trevino 12/39; **Jack Nicklaus 1/40**

42,43 Raymond Floyd 9/42

44-46 Tony Jacklin 7/44; Hale Irwin 6/45; David Graham 5/46

47,48 Johnny Miller 4/47; Larry Nelson 9/47

1949-1951 Tom Watson 9/49; Andy North 3/50; Fuzzy Zoeller 11/51

52,53 Ben Crenshaw 1/52

54-56 Curtis Strange 1/55; Greg Norman 2/55

57,58 M O'Meara; N Price 1/57; P Stewart 1/57; **Seve B 4/57; N Faldo 7/57**; B Langer 8/57; S Lyle, I Woosnam 2,3/58

1959-1961 Fred Couples 10/59

62,63 Vijay Singh 2/63; Colin Montgomerie 6/63

64-66 Davis Love III 4/64; Lee Janzen 8/64; Jose-Maria Olazabal 2/66; John Daly 4/66

67,68

1969-1971 Retief Goosen 2/69; Angel Cabrera 9/69; Ernie Els 10/69; Phil Mickelson 6/70; Padraig Harrington 8/71; David Duval 12/71

72,73

74-76 **Tiger Woods 12/75**

77,78

1979-1981

Chapter 10

Golf and Life

Many obvious advantages come from playing golf. A great one is that golf is quite a lot like Life, and so it is an excellent training for Life. Life has its ups and downs, and so does golf. In Life it is not so much how extreme and difficult are the ups and downs, but how we react to them. Much the same applies in golf. Golf can and should build character. We need to learn how to handle these different situations.

What are the main purposes of playing golf? To state the obvious, there is exercise, to build health and fitness; a challenge to improve, and increase our skill; pitting ourselves against others in competition and friendlies; fun and enjoyment, and several other reasons why one might want to play, such as social or business. I believe all these are very valid motives. But I think the *main* purpose should be to make new friends, and to cement existing friendships.

How do you do this? Every time you play, the priority should be to build a relationship with your playing partner(s) or opponent(s), whether it is a friendly or a competition or a desperately important match. You should do this while playing your best and hardest, but of course fairly in every way including heavier gamesmanship! You do this by being a pleasant and cheerful playing companion.

I have written in Chapter 4 "Managing your game", section 3 "How to handle your thought processes and keep your mind calm and working efficiently even when disaster strikes" of my recommendations for doing just that. I won't repeat them here, but summing up: Be a happy golfer; think of yourself as lucky (even if you don't sometimes); in a crisis, keep calm, and your mind unscrambled; try to see the funny side of desperate situations even as they are happening – it will put problems in perspective. All these lessons apply in much the same way in Life. Don't think too much about what's wrong with your life, your body or your golf, or what you can't do any more: think about what is right, and what you *can* still do – there are usually plenty of people less fortunate than oneself.

One of the worst golfing companions is a good golfer who let's everyone know that he shouldn't be playing as badly as this, and is too frequently incredulous and grumpy. Playing well below our best is a good test of character – we should try to turn it to advantage by remaining cheerful in these and other trying circumstances.

Playing in a medal competition can sometimes seem more like mental torment than pleasure. But why let this happen? A good attitude is to be eager to test yourself – both your golf and your mental resilience. If the golf goes badly, award yourself marks for whatever mental strength and enjoyment you can conjure up! Don't worry about your handicap going up one tenth of a shot – it should reflect how you've been playing. It's no good having a handicap that you can't play to!

Now follows a not entirely relevant piece, which

has its golfing connection. Winston Churchill is not remembered as a golfer, his golf doubtless over-shadowed by his painting and bricklaying, apart from his colossal achievements as statesman, historian and visionary. He played at Walton Heath, and is recorded * as declaring that "golf seems a good game for conversation". It is a surprise, Connelly continues, that James Braid gave Churchill the credit for inventing the "Greensome". Bernard Darwin failed to confirm this attribution, but was unable to establish any other contender. Churchill was arguably the greatest master of the English language, his only possible rival being Shakespeare, who did not put it to such practical use.

While on the subject of the Great Man, I would like to record my view of him, having read many books about him. I would think that while he had enough faults for half a dozen men, he had enough outstanding qualities for at least a dozen. I believe that no one in history has done remotely as much for so many in the free world, and that we owe him so much gratitude and appreciation.

On a lighter note, I am also a PG Wodehouse fan, in particular the Golf Omnibus with the Oldest Member, as those in my old school golfing society know. Was it PG who said, "If you want to get to know a man's character, play golf with him!"?

* *A Temple of Golf* – A History of a Woking Golf Club 1893–1993 by James Connelly.

Chapter 11

Some advantages of a brush with Cancer

On the face of it this is an absurd theme for a chapter in a golf book. Do skip this chapter if you don't like reading this sort of thing. But it is one I very much want to write, and I hope it will interest and help some readers. Everybody has some family or friends who have or have had problems with cancer, or another serious illness. Many people worry for others or for themselves about the possibility.

I am writing this chapter because I feel strongly, and because I am giving a substantial proportion of my sales from every book to the Cancer Research UK Charity. What I have to say is aimed at two main groups: (1) those who have had something nasty, and have been lucky enough to get over it, and (2) those for whom trouble recurs.

My story so far. I was found to have a sizeable lump in my bowel in April 2009, which was removed in May, and then from July I had nearly six months of chemotherapy, as the cancer had spread only a very small amount locally. Happily all the indications are good, and I will continue to be tested and checked for another four years.

A by-product of my cancer is this book. I was

lying awake one night in my study bed during a bad period of chemo, when I thought that with reduced activity it would be a chance to write down a few things that I had always meant to do for the few friends and grandchildren whom I had helped a bit with their golf. During these "lessons" I had told them a lot, and always meant to write it down, but never did. Writing this book has been therapeutic by giving me a project at a time when I couldn't get on with normal life.

How can there be advantages in cancer? I believe there are many. Here are some I can think of:

1   Doctors, surgeons and oncologists know a lot more about cancer these days, and with modern techniques they are getting pretty good at dealing with many types of cancer and curing them.

2   Nowadays you and your family and friends – anyone – can talk about it, which is a relatively recent development, and can be a great help.

3   You can get tremendous support and understanding from your friends and family and anyone you know.

4   Your family may come to appreciate you (even) more, realizing that you have something serious.

5   If you can have a positive attitude to it you will much improve your chances of beating it.

6   If you can have a positive cheerful attitude to it, you can set a wonderful example to others. Everyone who has not had cancer or another serious illness must worry from time to time that they might get something nasty. If you can show them that it does not have to affect their lives really badly, then you are doing something for humanity.

7   A great source of support and encouragement

can be from others, often friends, who have themselves been through it, and in many cases done well. With these "cancer friends" you can have a continuing close bond.

8   Chemo treatment need not be too bad. There is a chance that the first cycle (maybe three weeks or whatever) may be difficult. But the plan is to give you the right dose of treatment, which is meant to be manageable, not too uncomfortable, while still doing you a lot of good.

9   The level of pain you might suffer during and after an operation may not have to be very severe, thanks to pain-killing drugs.

10 If you are one of the many fortunate ones who gets over it, you should finish up with a new and better outlook on life, appreciating things more.

11 You can become a shade more outspoken in your opinions!

12 You or the person caring for you can more easily say, "I'm afraid I'm/he is tired, and need(s) to get some rest."

13 In the more difficult stages post-op and during and after chemo, you can get a good sleep in the afternoons – enjoy it!

14 I shouldn't say this, but you can possibly get away with slightly worse behavior than usual!

15 In hospital and afterwards you will have a lot of attention: some may enjoy this, others may not.

Some further suggestions:

16 Encourage openness with family and close friends - don't shut them out, including the children in the misguided belief that you are "sparing" them. Families and friends can have an

increased closeness when feeling part of a support team.

17 Do as much gentle exercise as you are advised you can safely manage - it should build you up not only physically, but improve your mental outlook.

18 Try to laugh as much as possible each day. If you are on "Sky", try G.O.L.D. – "Go on, laugh daily", or anything else that makes you laugh.

If you are unlucky, and have further problems, the chances are that because the specialists are getting so clever, they may well be able to overcome a recurrence with further treatment. If you are unlucky, or have a form of cancer which is currently incurable, you have every reason to be very down and anxious, as none of us wants to suffer and possibly die before our time. But I can still see some positives. Among these are:

1 Pain can probably be well controlled with drugs.

2 You have an opportunity to show all the people you know that illness, mental and physical suffering, and possibly untimely death need not be as horrible as it seems. By doing so, you can set an even more wonderful example to all those who know you, and an even greater service to humankind.

3 You could have the chance to really talk to your family and friends, and get to know sides of them, and they of you, that would otherwise not have been possible.

4 As time goes by, it seems that the Medical Profession is on the track of new cures for illnesses

which are currently incurable.

5   Clearly if you have firm religious beliefs it can
    help a lot. Having cancer might be a way to
    come by them, if you don't already have them.

Chapter 12

Creating your own short game course

If you have a garden or paddock, and some spare space in it, you might be able to create your own "Short Game Course". The smallest "Short Game Course" might just be one tee and one green: anything less would be a practice facility. Based on designing, helping build, and then maintaining my own tiny short game course, I can suggest ideas for making something out of a piece of ground much smaller than you might dream is possible.

I had a small area of sloping ground, and using less than half an acre I produced an 18-hole course by having five small greens and five tiny tees. Obviously the holes ran across each other, and so could not be played by a lot of people simultaneously. But I had various other circuits, including 9, 5 and 4 holes, and we used both the 5 and the 4 hole circuit around the perimeter for Charity days with up to 32 golfers in fourballs better-ball stableford. The total length of the 18 holes was 504.1 yards, an average of only 28 yards per hole, with the longest at 44.8 yards.

COMPETITION:						Par 46 & S.S.S. 46			
DATE:			TIME:				ENTRY No.		
	Name			Handicap	Strokes Recd	Divots	Over Fence		
Player A									
Player B									
Player C									
Player D									

Marker						Gross scores			Over	Points
D	Hole	Tee-Gr	Yards	Par	S.I	A	B	C	Divots	Fence	+ 0 -
	1	E - 2	22.1	2	18					
	2	B - 3	20.5	2	13					
	3	C - 4	19.5	3	4					
	4	D - 5	36.7	3	12					
	5	E - 4	32.2	3	7					
	6	D - 1	44.8	3	1					
	7	A - 3	29.1	2	15					
	8	C - 1	20.9	2	11					
	9	A - 5	26.9	3	5					
	OUT		252.7	23						

Marker						Gross scores			Over	Points
D	Hole	Tee-Gr	Yards	Par	S.I	A	B	C	Divots	Fence	+ 0 -
	10	E - 3	22.0	3	10					
	11	A - 2	18.0	2	16					
	12	B - 4	34.0	3	2					
	13	D - 3	22.2	2	17					
	14	C - 5	25.2	2	6					
	15	E - 1	27.7	3	8					
	16	A - 4	43.8	3	3					
	17	D - 2	32.6	2	14					
	18	B - 5	25.9	3	9					
	IN		251.4	23						
	OUT		252.7	23						
	TOTAL		504.1	46						
	STROKES RECD									
	NETT / PTS / HOLES									
DISTANCES are from tee centres to green centres						★ Different tee!				

Marker's signature .... Player's signature ....

Fig 12 Card of author's tiny short game course.

1 Greens

Greens were a mixture of bent grass and fescue. I used turf, but they could be from seed. Two were nearly 30 ft long by about 15 ft wide, and three were about 20ft x 15 ft. Four were flat – at that small size they had to be, and the larger fifth was a two-tier sloping green which also served as a practice green. One could not always have pitched or chipped to the greens satisfactorily if they had been of normal pace, which is about 6 to 11 on the Stimpmeter – as there would not have been enough space to stop most shots. Accordingly I kept them in the speed range 2.5 to 4, to make them receptive to high pitches from the tees and all shorter shots. I found that even at these grass lengths and slow speeds the ball would not hold on a slope of more than around 1 in 20.

2 Tees

Tees were built-up squares of grass just over 5 ft square, with an insert of artificial grass dead centre one foot square, from which you could either play off the artificial grass, or a tee peg within the one foot square. They were central to allow for left-handers.

3 Fairways

Fairways were simplified in my layout, by having four of the greens roughly in line, joined to each other by three fairways in line for economy of cutting most of the fairway area. I also had a few paths through the general rough, for walking, and for running a lower-flying chip along. Since fairway areas were so small, and would not stand many divots, I had a rule that divots were not allowed, and incurred a severe penalty. This gave rise to an alternative way of chipping – the "toed chip", which is very effective in avoiding divots, and works on your lawn, for the same reason. It is also a very useful method to have in your armoury on the actual golf course, as described in Chapter 6 "Chipping", sections 4.2.3 and 4, having a number of advantages over the standard square chip. You place the ball very much closer to your right foot, by making the club shaft almost vertical, and so the part of the club which contacts the ground is smoothly rounded and much smaller than the long sole in the standard square chip. This greatly reduces resistance on contact with the ground, and the likelihood of a fluff or double hit, and other problems.

4 Bunkers

I had two, partly as hazards, partly for practice (one was long, to prevent sand being splashed out, and partly to stop the ball from running into some bushes).

5 Hole strategies

My 18 holes were arranged so that they could all be played in three different ways: (1) with a high stopping lob landing on the green, or (2) with a high pitch landing near the green whether on fairway or in rough with a calculated kick onto the green, or (3) with a lower runner, all along the fairway or cut paths.

6 Number of greens

A Short Game course needs to have at least one green. If it has a single green only, it gives you a chance to have a really good green, of more like normal size and appropriate speed, and it can be designed to be approached from at least two different tees. The green(s) will need some fairway round it/them, and at least one bunker would be handy. Another arrangement might be say three greens and three tees, which could give nine different holes, playing from each tee to all greens, especially if no tee is too near any green. Of course extra tees are much easier to make, if they are of my simple construction as 5 ft squares, and six tees + three greens could give you your 18 holes. Fig 12 shows the card I made for my tiny 18-hole Short Game course.

7 Artificial grass

There are companies that will sell you artificial greens, and I imagine they also have artificial aprons and fairways, and sections of fairway-length artificial grass from which to chip or pitch. For a Short Game course the chances are that virtually all of it would be of natural grass, but the main green, which might be your only green, could be of artificial grass. Either way it could double up as a practice putting and chipping green. I don't know how realistically the bounce reacts on an artificial green, but I believe that some pros have them, and they probably are realistic, and need less maintenance.

Chapter 13

Golf at Home

The previous Chapter 12 described what you might do by way of a very simple or more complex Short Game course in your own garden or grounds. Most people will not want to do this, or will feel they don't have the space. For such golfers who don't want to go that far, but want to do something by way of practice and/or loosening up, and/or making some of the golf movements at home, here are some suggestions. They fall under two main headings:

1 Practice outdoors

Ideas include:

1.1 A practice net

Must be safe from any mishit, including the dread shank! This could involve extra side nets to catch the worst case shank, especially if you have neighbours, or any of the public who might conceivably be in range. The advantage is that you are hitting actual shots, and can get a good idea of the quality of your contact, while working your golf muscles.

1.2 Real shots

Hit real shots onto your own ground, only provided it is 100% safe, including mishits. Chances are you might be limited to fairly short shots by the length available or by losing balls in long grass or bushes. But something is better than nothing.

1.3   Create your own green

Create your own green and/or bunker. Chapter 12 "Your own short game course" decribes what you can do about constructing greens. The green could either be real grass, or artificial grass, likely to be very expensive, but less maintenance, and more durable. Chipping onto the green could be from normal lawn grass, or possibly an artificial grass. In either case some slopes both from the apron and the green itself would be much more useful than general flatness.

1.4   Chip on your lawn

Chapter 6 "Chipping" describes different techniques: to preserve your lawn without taking divots out of it, use the "toed" chipping method – see 6.4.2.3 and 4 in Chapter 6, with the shaft almost vertical, and only a very small amount of your iron in contact with the ground. By doing this, you will minimize the chance of a divot which would be much more likely using the conventional method, where the club's entire sole touches the ground.

1.5   Mirrors

If possible have a large mirror (not easy), so that you can see yourself swing from one or two angles. If not a mirror, a large plate-glass window may do the trick. Failing that, look at your shadow to see how much your head moves during the swing – it should move a modest amount each way. If you have a mirror, you could mark on it with permanent or removable markers, straight lines showing the angles for 30, 60 90, and 120 degrees say to give you a better feeling for how far back you have gone. These angles would particularly help your part-strength wedges.

1.6 Filming

Get yourself filmed with a camcorder or videocamera. I don't know to what extent you can get good quality slow-motion with modern equipment, but clearly the better the quality and the more pictures per second, the more you will be able to see.

2 Practice indoors

Ideas include:

2.1 Putting

Any carpet will do. Speed or slowness do not matter, because one quickly adapts to extreme changes of pace ranging from 2 to 20 + on the Stimpmeter. Slopes do not matter – on the contrary, it is much better if you have an old house with good borrows, provided your carpet is not too quick. For a hole you could buy a real golf hole, and you might be able to let it into your floorboards – easier if you are building from new. Therefore not many will want to do this. An alternative that is better anyway is to buy a thin, slightly flexible rubber disc, readily available to make opening stiff jars easier, usually 4.9" in diameter. Sections 9.1 and 2 of Chapter 5 – "Putting" describe how you can use this disc, with a simple length of string, to learn a lot about how to deal with the vital short putts up to 6 feet. If you have plenty of space you can practise longer putts too. If directional accuracy is a problem with longer putts, you can put a cushion about 10 feet away, and hit the ball with a fuller putting swing, noting deviation from target.

2.2 Chipping

There is plenty of scope, but you may need to take precautions against bangings and damage which may upset your household or neighbours. This can usually be done by various cushions and possibly heavy curtains. This chipping practice can be valuable when trying to ingrain a new chipping movement.

2.3 Pitching

The scope for pitching is clearly smaller, but it is not impossible.

2.4 Full practice swings

Clearly good headroom is needed – at least 10' as mentioed above for a driver. To reduce headroom needed by 9" or so, use a wedge. A child's wedge would give a further reduction as would gripping down. If you have a low ceiling, you could get a sawn-off regripped club, but they don't give the right feel.

2.5 Practice net

It would be ideal, as it doesn't depend on weather and daylight, but very few people are likely to have the space and facilities. If you do, it is vital to cover all possible complete mishits and safety hazards, with the ball flying around at high speed indoors!

2.6 Mirrors

Indoors there can be more scope for seeing yourself swing via mirrors at the front and side, each useful, and the same mirror might be used for both. Another handy aid is to mark onto the mirror lines showing various angles of say 30, 60, 90 and 120 degrees for part-strength wedges.

2.7 Filming

Camcorders tolerate poor light conditions, and so can be used indoors easily. See also outdoor filming above re slow motion.

Chapter 14

The Older Golfer

Golf is in at least one way the greatest of the physical games, in that you can keep at it until a ripe old age, injuries and bad luck with your health permitting. Keeping on playing golf will improve your chance of keeping going. Some of the benefits of golf are outlined in Chapter 10 – "Golf and Life". Foremost can be physical and mental well-being, and camaraderie among your friends, old and new. But common to many golfers is the desire to improve, to reduce the rate of decline, and to be not too bad for one's age.

The handicap is an indispensible way of producing a level playing field. Most golfers doubtless yearn or have yearned to get down to an impressively low handicap. But it's not much good having a low handicap if you can't really play to it. For the ageing golfer there is another yardstick as well – to be good for your age. This implies being reasonably fit and healthy, so that you can get round the course, and also having some skill. Both these things can be worked on and improved.

I don't know how many scratch events there are for "Seniors" over certain ages. Some, e.g. the National Amateur Seniors Championships, usually start at 55, and have supplementary categories at five-year intervals to produce something of a level playing field. There are also events (e.g. the Bernard Darwin competitions) for Old Boys from certain schools, covering age groups from 55, 65 and 75 playing scratch foursomes match-play in teams of six for four rounds in two days (75s play a single stableford round.) The main event for the 75 and overs is scratch, but there is also a handicap event, based solely on age, not handicap. In all these events there is a premium on good golf for your age.

In an attempt to improve standards among older old boys at my school, I recently introduced a special scratch salver, played in conjunction with the main stableford handicap event, the latter producing qualifiers for the match-play cups that follow. I tried to get as level a playing field as possible for the entire field of all ages from about 18 up to men into their 90s. I did this by taking a hypothetical good golfer of around 3 handicap in his prime, and then estimated with much deliberation what handicap he would be at all older ages, assuming he kept it going. I concluded that he would start to fall off a bit from around 55, with increases in handicap with the years, at first slow, but then quickening, before settling down to around one shot a year. The number of extra points added needs to be slightly less than the notional handicap increases, because one point is worth slightly more than one stroke, especially in a scratch event.

Fig 14 shows for all ages from 54 upwards how I believe an average good golfer's handicap should go up with increasing age up to 95. It also shows how many extra stableford points should be added to his scratch stableford score in a competition of this type. There are two further complications. First, from the age of 80 players should have the choice of going off a designated forward tee if they wish, either every time, or whenever they choose.

Second, there is a risk is that the weather may be ghastly, particularly at a seaside course, with wind gusts up to force 8 (which I reckon is not far off an 8-club wind), and lashing rain. In this case a winning score in the main stableford handicap competition may be as low as around 15 pts, or even a lot less than 15 in the scratch section, and the 90-year-old with 17 pts added needn't go out – clearly absurd. And so I added an adjustment for bad or awful weather. If the average of the four best scores in the main stableford handicap is 35 pts or better, then full extra pts are added. But for every 5 pt reduction in the average of the four best scores, the points added are reduced by 10%. For example if the average of the four best scores in the main competition is 15.0 to 19.9 points, the points added will be reduced to 60% of standard.

To get the winner of the Age-adjusted Scratch Stableford, you take the scratch stableford scores and add extra points for those over 54. It is not nearly as hard as it seems, because the first rough check is to deduct handicaps from the handicap points, and then add extra points, to give a rough calculation. This will leave you with a small number of cards to look at closely.

Fig 14 – Target handicaps and Points added for "good" golfers over 54 years.

Age of golfer	Target handicap for "good" golfer	Stableford points to be added to scratch stableford score
18-54	3	0
55-59	4	1
60-64	5	2
65-67	6	3
68-70	7	4
71,72	8	5
73,74	9	6
75,76	10	7
77,78	11	8
79, 80 Forward tee option at 80	12	9
81	13	10
82	14	10
83	15	11
84	16	12
85	17	13
86	18	13
87	19	14
88	20	15
89	21	16
90	22	17
91	23	17
92	24	18
93	25	19
94	26	20
95	27	21

There is no reason why the two entirely separate and different competitions cannot be run concurrently, as we do at my school autumn meeting. The entire field will be competitive in the normal Stableford Handicap, but in the Age-Adjusted Scratch event, golfers under 55 on higher handicaps, and older golfers who are not reasonably good for their age will not be as competitive.

I don't know whether many golf clubs, societies or County Unions operate or have thought of doing something similar. An Age-Adjusted Scratch Stableford could be run either (1) as an event on its own, in which case it would attract mainly better golfers of all ages, or (2) as my school does it, with two simultaneous events, also for all ages.

There is a third option – to cater only for 55 and over, and this could either be scratch only, or scratch plus handicap. There would probably not be enough support at the club level, but there may be enough numbers at the County or National level.

Appendix for Chapter 3

Common Conceptions questioned CC 4 and CC 5

This appendix discusses in some depth these two closely related topics, with further detail to the brief summaries of CC 4 "Clubhead speed alone determines distance", and CC 5 "After impact nothing can change the outcome" in Chapter 3.

Both maxims are strongly stated in the exceptionally influential and generally excellent book *The Search for the Perfect Swing* 1968 (SPS) which was reprinted in 2005 with a new updating preface by the main original scientific author, the texts being unchanged. The two topics are very closely inter-related, and can be considered both separately and together: they are two sides of the same coin. The first, "clubhead speed alone ...", could be thought of as what happens up to impact. SPS appears to mean initial impact. The second maxim, "after impact nothing can change the outcome" clearly should refer to what happens after the ball has been launched into free flight. SPS appears to have researched and referred to only a teed-up driver or wood shot. SPS makes these statements, among others:

1. "The only dynamic factor that matters in producing distance is clubhead speed. A clubhead making square contact with the ball at 100 miles per hour will send it the same distance whether it is accelerating, slowing down, or moving at constant speed." This statement supports the first maxim, CC 4.

2. "The whole effective part of a stroke is com-

pleted before the golfer hits the ball; thus any energy not already by then slung into the club-head is powerless to affect the shot in any way whatsoever." This statement more or less supports the second, CC 5, and also reinforces the first, CC 4. There are other variables, see below, which can affect distance possibly a lot more.

I do not quite agree with the SPS statement No.1 re CC 4 because I believe there must be a difference, however small, between a clubhead which continues to be driven by the golfer, and one that is genuinely "freewheeling", or being driven less. However, after much thought, and investigation, including talks with a leading club manufacturer, I believe their statement is not far from correct in the case of a teed-up driver or wood, but it is not quite the whole story. The club manufacturer was inclined to agree with my theories, but was unwilling to support them because they had not researched this particular question sufficiently. I believe that club manufacturers have not looked deeply into this question because (a) research is not easy, and (b) my logic may well be of limited importance compared with other variables at impact such as off-centre contact. In engineering terms, the net energy applied to the ball, which is the accurate measure of its launch speed, is proportional to the net work done on the ball. This is correctly defined as the mean net force applied to the ball times the distance over which that force acts. SPS believes that from the moment of initial impact the clubhead can no longer apply much effective further force to the ball, because the clubhead acts as if it were a loose mass, connected to the shaft and player as if by string. Therefore any further "drive" through the ball during the very short period of impact can have very little or no effect on the ball. They go further by saying that any extra energy applied is effectively wasted. I believe that the SPS scientific reasoning for justifying their theories are not quite as rigorous as the many other excellent items of research throughout their work. Since my reasons for holding that belief would take more lengthy explanation, I will not devote yet more space here.

However, I believe that they would accept, although they have not said so in the book, that a high clubhead speed at impact or initial impact can be achieved only if the follow-through is "good and full". I now believe that the difference between my position and SPS is probably small, and could be thought of as academic for a teed-up wood. However I believe there is another case, which SPS have not written about, which is different, and must be mentioned. This is the iron shot which takes a divot. As outlined in CC 4 in Chapter 3, this case is different in two ways – there is more resistance from the turf, and less flexing of the shaft, which should mean that the clubhead can be driven through the ball more than in the case of the driver.

As I have said in Chapter 3 itself, there are other factors at work which probably have a much larger effect on distance, including the degree of off-centre impact, launch angle, spin rate, clubhead path, shaft flex and torsion and ball (and clubhead) compression. I believe the reason that the question of clubhead dynamics before, during and after impact have not been investigated to anything like the same degree seems to me to be that the outcomes of variations in the latter are of a substantially smaller order, and therefore of less significance. When I started this particular quest for the truth about club-head speed, I was under the impression that a slower or medium speed swing with good acceleration or drive through the ball was better for good distance and accuracy than a faster swing with little continuing drive. I have changed my view to come closer to the SPS view, but subject to reservations. I now believe that the effect of continuing to drive through the ball during and after impact may be very small in itself, although I believe it does exist. But far more important: without a positive drive through, one cannot achieve one's fastest club-head speed, and with it maximum distance.

I believe that this debate, which is somewhat academic in the case of the teed-up driver, will be proved one day, not easily, but it can be done in two ways. First with driving machines in which the continuing application of power over and above "free-wheeling" into impact can be varied, and the outcomes measured. Alternatively or additionally with real golfers where the swing is filmed at modestly high speeds of around 10,000 pictures per second, to see how varying velocity patterns before, during and after impact affect the outcomes of distance and accuracy. To determine what happens during the very short impact phase, higher speeds around 100,000 pictures per second are needed, well within the capacity of modern digital cameras, to check shaft flex and twist, and driver face and ball compression. Natural frequencies of shaft flexion and twist may also be factors.

Publisher's note

For reference to specific aspects of technical and non-technical content, the reader should turn to the detailed contents pages v–ix at the beginning of the book.